Dear Reader:

The book you are about to read is the latest bestseller from the St. Martin's True Crime Library, the imprint the *New York Times* calls "the leader in true crime!" Each month, we offer you a fascinating account of the latest, most sensational crime that has captured the national attention. St. Martin's is the publisher of perennial bestselling true crime author Jack Olsen whose SALT OF THE EARTH is the true story of one woman's triumph over life-shattering violence; Joseph Wambaugh called it "powerful and absorbing." Fannie Weinstein and Melinda Wilson tell the story of a beautiful honors student who was lured into the dark world of sex for hire in THE COED CALL GIRL MURDER. St. Martin's is also proud to publish critically acclaimed author Carlton Stowers, whose 1999 Edgar Award-winning TO THE LAST BREATH recounts a two-year-old girl's mysterious death, and the dogged investigation that led loved ones to the most unlikely murderer: her own father. In the book you now hold, MURDER AT YOSEMITE, veteran reporter and bestselling author Carlton Smith looks at a series of brutal murders at one of our most famous national parks, a case that has received international attention.

St. Martin's True Crime Library gives you the stories *behind* the headlines. Our authors take you right to the scene of the crime and into the minds of the most notorious murderers to show you what really makes them tick. St. Martin's True Crime Library paperbacks are better than the most terrifying thriller, because it's all true! The next time you want a crackling good read, make sure it's got the St. Martin's True Crime Library logo on the spine—you'll be up all night!

Charles E. Spicer, Jr.
Senior Editor, St. Martin's True Crime Library

Yosemite: for most of his life, it seemed, Yosemite had been some sort of lodestone, subtly drawing him, or at least influencing his fortunes and that of his poor, tattered, tragic family. Who knew what the place's power was, or where it came from? But it called to him, summoned him, in a deep way he did not completely fathom. It was light, it was air, it was darkness; and in some part of his mind, the killer knew the park was menace, although he could never explain how, or why. It was freedom, and it was nature; and true nature was as savage as it was unpredictable.

As he was . . .

—from *Murder at Yosemite*

ST. MARTIN'S PAPERBACKS TRUE CRIME LIBRARY TITLES BY CARLTON SMITH

Blood Money

Death of a Little Princess

Seeds of Evil

Dying for Daddy

Death in Texas

Murder at Yosemite

Murder at
Yosemite

Carlton Smith

St. Martin's Paperbacks

MURDER AT YOSEMITE

Copyright © 1999 by Carlton Smith.

Cover photograph of Cary Stayner courtesy AP/Wide World Photos. Cover photograph of Yosemite National Park © Darrell Gulin/Tony Stone Images.

ISBN: 0-312-97457-4

Printed in the United States of America

St. Martin's Paperbacks edition / November 1999

St. Martin's Paperbacks are published by St. Martin's Press, 175 Fifth Avenue, New York, NY 10010.

10 9 8 7 6 5 4 3 2 1

AUTHOR'S NOTE AND ACKNOWLEDGMENTS

Yosemite National Park remains one of the nation's greatest natural treasures: a huge expanse of fragile alpine wilderness, spectacular gray granite escarpments, majestic waterfalls descending thousands of feet to a valley floor so pristine that its earliest visitors considered it the closest thing to Eden left on Earth. Each year, nearly four million people visit the park for camping, hiking, swimming and rock climbing; many, in fact, do little more than gape at the awesome scenery, one of nature's monuments to the power of the planet to create and redefine itself over the eons of its existence.

The abrupt, mysterious disappearance of three women among those four million annual visitors in the early months of 1999 transfixed two nations; it wasn't just that they vanished without any reasonable explanation, although that was peculiar enough. It was the fact that they had disappeared at the very doorstep of one of the country's most impressive symbols of our civility, an outdoor wonderland where usually the most threatening reality is the prospect of hungry bears conducting car prowls for inadequately sealed sack lunches, or the occasional traffic jam.

But the vanishing of Carole Sund, Juliana Sund, and Silvina Pelosso during the night of February 15, 1999 from a motel at the park's gateway raised the prospect of another, far more deadly threat; violence of man against woman, and in such a place of beauty it seemed particularly obscene. And because of the nature of the victims—innocents, people who had done nothing more than attempt to enjoy themselves while basking in nature's glory, just as millions before them had and will again—America turned its collective eye on Yosemite Park and wondered: would it ever be safe to go to any of our national parks again?

As an FBI agent later put the events in perspective, Carole, Juli, and Silvina represented good, people doing innocent, happy things; and the very fact that they had fallen victim to random, mindless violence struck a chord in all of us. In the most visceral way, it told us that none of us was truly safe, no matter where we were. In short, what had happened to Carole, Juli, and Silvina could have happened to any of us, and it made us all recoil.

It was the peculiar nature of Carole, Juli, and Silvina's disappearance that was to affect the events that followed. One evening they were there, doing normal things, eating hamburgers and watching videos; the next morning they were simply gone, along with all their luggage and their rented car. No one knew what in the beginning, the news media's subsequent criticism of the agency was to seen a bit jaundiced. In truth, given the circumstances it initially faced, the FBI did pretty much all it could do. It was only after specific evidence was developed that a viable pathway of investigation emerged. That the pathway led publicly to a series of suspects who may not have been directly involved in the events was simply thorough police work, and an investigative tack that would have been taken by any law enforcement agency in America, given the circumstances; that the names and the focus of the investigation became public, and the public was led to believe that a resolution was at hand was far more the result of news media excesses in the climate that had previously been created than it was the fault of the FBI. As the FBI repeatedly pointed out, it wasn't they who named names and advanced theories as to what had happened; instead it was the news media, caught in the ever-shortening gap between rumor and the rush to report.

Indeed, given the lengths the confessed perpetrator went to in covering up his crimes, it is doubtful that any solution would have been possible to the disappearance of Carole, Juli, and Silvina, except through events surrounding a later murder: that of park naturalist Joie Armstrong. It was Joie's stout if futile resistance to her attacker that made the solution to the crimes finally possible. In that sense, Joie Armstrong stands as the real heroine of the murders at Yosemite.

Special thanks are due here to a variety of individuals who significantly assisted in the preparation of this had happened to them, and there was not a shred of visible evidence left behind to hint at their fate.

The complete absence of any clue as to what had befallen the trio in turn prompted law enforcement to adopt unusual tactics. Pressed by the families of the missing to mount an all-out search, augmented by monetarily significant rewards, the Federal Bureau of Investigation actively sought the assistance of the public in helping to develop leads. That, in turn led to an unusually cooperative relationship between the FBI and the news media, at least at the beginning. Indeed, the way the disappearance of the trio and the subsequent events unfolded is as much a story of the relationship between law enforcement and the news purveyors as it is a story about an investigation's progress and the dreadful events that were subsequently revealed. For that reason, this book stands as much as a critique of the performance of the news media as it does an accounting of the events that ended in tragedy.

Because of this, I have tried as much as possible to explain not only the events surrounding the disappearances, but also the reasonings behind the FBI's actions, as well as those of the news media; indeed, the two all-too-often mixed together, at times with good results, and at others with ill.

After the awful truth of what happened was revealed, the FBI and other law enforcement agencies came in for considerable criticism, much of it from the formerly cooperative news media, for a number of decisions and assumptions that were made during the investigation. Having relied upon the FBI as their primary authority accounting: Charles Spicer, my editor at St. Martin's Press, was as helpful and supportive in this project as he has always been with others, and under the particularly difficult circumstances of a story that was still unfolding even as it was being written. So too, was Joe Cleemann of St. Martin's Press, whose assistance in arranging the often arcane logistical details is gratefully appreciated. Jane Dystel of Jane Dystel Literary Management was instrumental in the arrangements that made this accounting possible, and I thank her as well.

Additionally, the help of former Merced Police officers Jerry Price and Gary Starbuck was invaluable in helping reconstruct the quarter-century-old events that played such a significant role in the eventual disappearance of Carole, Juli, and Silvina. Television reporter Ted Rowlands of Bay Area stations KNTV and KBWB provided vital insight into the circumstances of his exclusive jailhouse interview with Cary Stayner; indeed, Rowlands's dogged persistence in the performance of his job despite repeated rebuffs stands as an outstanding example of journalistic enterprise.

Finally, let me express grateful appreciation to Marvin, Margit, and Erica Stuart of Madera County, whose support at a difficult time in the preparation of this book was instrumental in its completion.

Carlton Smith
San Francisco, California
September, 1999

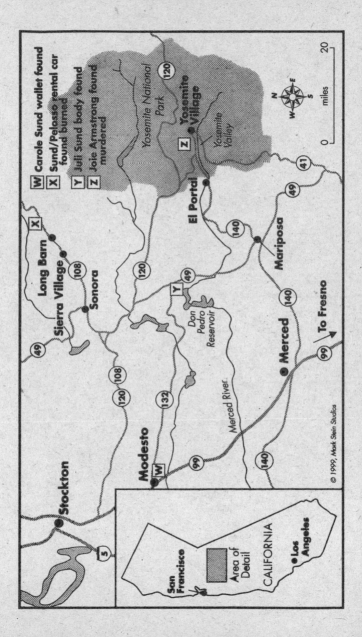

W Carole Sund wallet found
X Sund/Pelosso rental car found burned
Y Juli Sund body found
Z Joie Armstrong found murdered

Stockton

Modesto
W

Merced

To Fresno

Long Barn
X
Sierra Village
Sonora

Mariposa

El Portal

Yosemite Village
Z
Yosemite National Park
Yosemite Valley

Don Pedro Reservoir
Y

Merced River

0   20
miles

N
W   E
S

5
99
108
120
132
140
49
41
49
140

© 1999, Mark Stein Studios

San Francisco

Area of Detail

CALIFORNIA

Los Angeles

Murder at
Yosemite

PROLOGUE

THE KILLER KNEW HIS TERRAIN. For several years he had studied it, observing those who checked in and checked out, as they unpacked and repacked the trunks of their cars, changing clothes, showering—he liked to think about that—then dining in the restaurant, so clean, so fresh, so . . . youthful. The next day they'd drive into the park; maybe he'd see them again, but probably not.

They were part of the landscape, the brown young girls with their backpacks, their finely toned muscles, their energy. They came and they went; it didn't matter, really. In some ways they were all the same, even as their clothes and colors changed; they were innocent, which was what he craved. He knew what his secret heart desired, even if he couldn't tell another soul.

The sprawling lodge was almost like home to the killer. He knew its geography like he knew his own body. There was the main administration building with its lobby and gift shop; there was the restaurant and bar, with the glittering blue pool behind, in summer always worth watching. There were the sprawling, box-like complexes of rooms, upstairs and down, 206 in all, in six separate buildings inching up the slope toward the mountain behind.

And across the highway was the river. Rushing through its narrow canyon, bouncing over arrays of broken granite slabs and stones, the Merced was a constant, almost living thing: bright, merry, mischievous in its own way, the world's largest gravel-making machine. On its banks, shaded by trees, one could find a hidden beach, where one could strip off everything, and try to become one with the mystical landscape.

All in all, the killer loved El Portal: there was work, there were familiar faces, there was a sense of security, a place that had become home. He might be faceless, but he was the permanent one, the one who was there year-round, just like the gigantic gray cliff faces in the awesome park farther up the bouncing river: Yosemite.

Yosemite: for most of his life, it seemed, Yosemite had been some sort of lodestone, subtly drawing him, or at least influencing his fortunes and that of his poor, tattered, tragic family. Who knew what the place's power was, or where it came from? But it called to him, summoned him, in a deep way he did not completely fathom. It was light, it was air, it was darkness; and in some part of his mind, the killer knew the park was menace, although he could never explain how, or why. It was freedom, and it was nature; and true nature was as savage as it was unpredictable.

As he was . . .

* * *

You could drive into the park—it almost seemed sac-
riligious to call it a park when it had nothing in common with the tamed swatches of greenified ground that
most Americans called parks—and almost immediately
be overwhelmed by the grandeur of the bowl of the
valley, surrounded on all sides by towering cliffs, decorated by enormous waterfalls descending thousands of
feet to the valley floor. It was why the tourists came,
of course, nearly 4 million each year. Every day, tens
of thousands streamed up the narrow road along the
banks of the Merced, and into the canyon, by bus, by
car, by bicycle, even on foot. And all of them gawked,
craning their necks at the gigantic cliffs and the waterfalls that glistened down their sheer faces.

In his mind, the rubberneckers were trespassers, an
evil necessary for him to survive, to live, but seen as
a temporary infestation of the true park, the true beauty
of the valley. In a way, the tourists were nothing more
than moving objects, and unnatural ones at that. He had
the same sort of feeling for the visitors that one might
have for a herd of cattle that belonged to someone else.

None of them knew, or would ever understand, what
Yosemite meant to him. It was seared in his soul, and
would always be so tied up in the pain, the guilt, the
anger, the sorrow of his life that no one would ever
guess at the forces raging inside of his placid exterior.
It went back a long way.

**MERCED, CALIFORNIA
DECEMBER 4, 1972**

ONE

A Monday afternoon, cloudy, sometimes rainy, altogether too cold. Overnight, an Arctic front of frozen air had rushed down into California's Central Valley, plunging temperatures on the ground into the low forties. Little Steven Stayner, seven years old, was on his way home from school as the twilight gathered and the icy wind picked up. No one gave much attention to the second-grader as he made his way on a familiar shortcut past a service station on Yosemite Parkway toward the familiar house on Betty Street, where Steven lived with his mother Kay, father Del, and four brothers and sisters. Other things were happening in the world that day, some of vital interest to many nations, still others that would loom even larger to one nation in the months to come.

Halfway around the world from that gray December day in the small valley town of Merced—"mercy" in Spanish—a man named Henry Kissinger was sitting across a negotiating table with a Vietnamese diplomat named Le Duc Tho; both men were trying to fashion an agreement that would bring more than a decade's fruitless, bloody war to an end, a conflict that had transfixed the nation as no other in a generation.

Far less noticed was the action taken in a federal court in Washington, D.C., where a judge was sowing the seeds for the eventual destruction of a presidency.

"This jury," said Chief U.S. District Court Judge John J. Sirica, "is going to want to know, what did these men go into that headquarters for? Was the sole purpose political espionage? Was there financial gain? Who hired them? Who started this?" And with those questions, still not completely answered even today, Judge Sirica set into motion the events that would eventually cause the scandal called Watergate.

Those were two of the largest events of the times, more than a generation removed from where we are today; the fate of a small boy in a small town would gather comparatively little notice, for all its tragic consequences so many years later.

Little Steven turned toward home, a warm, welcoming cocoon just three blocks away. Out of the corner of his vision he saw a nondescript, gray van pull up on the street beside him. A small man got out, holding what looked to be religious leaflets. Would Steven's mother be willing to make a donation to the church? the man asked. Steven didn't see any reason why not. After all, the Stayner family was always willing to help others in need, that was just the way they lived. The little man offered to give Steve a ride home. Steven got in the van. It was the last time anyone saw a boy named Steven Stayner for more than seven long years.

Just what happened to Steven on that cold day in December in 1972 could only be pieced together later—much later—drawing on Steven's understandbly cloudy memory, and the recollections of those who made Steven himself the "donation" they sought.

Steven recalled that aside from the little man who had first approached him with the leaflets asking about a donation, there was a second man in the van, this one behind the wheel. This man was larger and older than the little man, and seemed to be in charge. Steven soon learned that the older man's name was Ken. Ken drove the van farther and farther away from Betty Street and Steve's house; he told Steve they would soon telephone Kay to let her know everything was okay.

Sometime that evening, in fact, Ken did stop the van, and made a telephone call. It's all right, he assured Steve after hanging up. Your mom knows you're with us, and she says it's all right if you go with us. After that, things became hazy to Steven; it was difficult to stay awake and alert; he drifted in and out as the van drove on through the night, tires rhythmically humming over the narrow asphalt roads. Over low hills, past barren fields, on into the night toward a destination Steve could only wonder about—when he had the energy to think.

Dawn came, and Steven found himself with the two men in some sort of trailer home, a place he'd never seen before. Now Ken explained everything to him:

Steven was to go with Ken from now on: Steve's mother Kay and father Del didn't want him anymore, they couldn't afford him. In fact, Ken said, a court had awarded custody of Steven to him, and from now Ken would take care of him. Still, Steve felt disoriented, drowsy; was it really possible that he wasn't wanted by his mother and father? What had he done to make them not want him? But in his disoriented condition, anything seemed possible. Steven went back to sleep, and when he awoke again, the van was on the move once more.

For Kay and Del Stayner, the first inkling that something had happened to their seven-year-old came the evening of December 4, when Steven never made it home from school.

After the usual calls to neighbors and Steven's playmates, the Stayners called the Merced Police Department to report Steven missing. The department put out the word to patrol officers to be watchful for a wandering seven-year-old. When the morning of the fifth came without Steven having been found, the officers of the department had to confront the likelihood that little Steven Stayner had been abducted. So, too, did Kay and Del Stayner. Who could have done such a thing? Given the Stayner family's financial circumstances— Del was a maintenence worker at a Merced-area food cannery—ransom was almost certainly not the motive.

For the Merced authorities assigned to investigate the case, the prospects of Steven's longterm survival appeared grim. Every year across the United States,

Sergeant Bill Bailey knew, hundreds of children Steven's age simply vanished, the all-too-vulnerable prey of traveling pedophiles. By far the most common outcome of such abductions was repeated rape, followed by abrupt homicide, covered up by a shallow grave that most likely would never be discovered. Indeed, it was the lucky ones whose graves were found; most such victims were never heard from again.

Because the town of Merced—then about 35,000 residents—was located on one of California's major north-south highway connectors, U.S. 99, the possibility that Steven might be hundreds of miles away from home within just a few hours of his disappearance was quite real. Major roads from Merced lead in every direction—south to Los Angeles, east to San Jose and San Francisco, north to Sacramento and Oregon, and east to Yosemite and Reno and places still farther away.

The first task was to canvass the route Steven normally used when walking home from school. But interviews with residents along the streets turned up nothing.

If the kidnapping wasn't for ransom—that seemed unlikely, since Del and Kay hardly had the kind of money to make it worthwhile—the most likely motive for the kidnapping was sexual. To cover that possibility, someone pulled the records of known sex offenders in the Merced area, and prepared to interview them.

Flyers with Steven's photograph and the circumstances of his disappearance were distributed, and publicity was arranged in the local news media. A check

of traffic and parking citations was made on out-of-area
vehicles with the idea that some known pedophile may
have been passing through Merced at the time Steven
disappeared. Finally, Bailey and his subordinates put
out the word on the national law enforcement system's
Teletype: boy missing; please call if located; please call
if any homicide victim matches our description.

Only someone who has experienced the unexplained
disappearance of a child can imagine the feelings of a
couple like Del and Kay Stayner in the days and weeks
after December 4, 1972. A day that had begun as normally as any other in a cheerful, well-adjusted household had, by nightfall become a frightening, nearly
unfathomable threat. Even the darkness and chill
seemed malevolent.

Was Steven lost? Was he hurt? Was he hungry?
Cold? Frightened? Was he in pain? No matter how
calm reason told the Stayners to be, those and other
questions stabbed repeatedly into their thoughts. Where
was their seven-year-old? The very absence of information magnified the fears and the pain of the Stayners,
who wavered between the hope that somehow Steven
would miraculously turn up, and the despair that even
as they waited, someone, somewhere was doing horrible things to their son, things they were helpless to
prevent.

At first, Kay was afraid to leave the house, for fear
that Steven or someone might call with information on
his whereabouts. The not knowing was driving her

crazy; Del took to driving around the streets and highways near Merced, looking for clues to his son's disappearance, a loaded shotgun beside him on the seat.

The very uncertainty of the event, surrounded as it was by phantasms of trauma imagined and the impossibility of repressing hope, transformed the Stayner family overnight; things would never be the same as they had been before December 4. In a matter of hours, Del and Kay were transmuted from the supporters of their children to victims; and the remaining children were subtly altered into the supporters of their parents—a difficult transition for anyone, but arduously hard for four normal preteens with their own needs. At one stroke, the missing Steven had become the missing center of his family, the black hole around which everyone and everything else revolved, and for which there were no answers.

Indeed, for Del and Kay to look at the others—oldest son Cary, 11, and the three youngest—was to wonder: whatever had happened to Steven? What would Steven be doing now, if *it*, whatever it was, had never happened?

Steven became the unmentionable wound at the center of the Stayner family, the gaping hole in the fabric of their relations; in some ways, at least initially, it would have been kinder if Steven's body had been found, because at least that way, the family could go on. But the blank wall of information about his fate, as if he existed and then ceased to exist for no apparent reason, loomed ever larger in the Stayner household:

something not to talk about because talking about it didn't do any good, but something never to forget, even as the years unfolded without a single clue as to whatever had happened.

TWO

THE WEEK OF CHRISTMAS OF 1972 found Steven Stayner sharing a small cabin in Yosemite Valley with Ken and his small friend. Most of the time, Steven stayed inside with either Ken or the small man, who seemed to take turns going out for hours and then coming back. It snowed much of the time, and while Steve wasn't exactly sure where he was, he guessed that he was somewhere in the mountains. From remarks made by Ken and the small man, Steven guessed they were in Yosemite; he was slightly familiar with the park, because his grandfather lived there.

But where in the park? The place was huge, Steven knew. Somehow, Steven learned or guessed that Ken and his little friend had something to do with the main lodge in the center of the park. But Steven wasn't sure exactly where it was, or how to get there. The cold weather, the snow, and the fact that he was kept under nearly constant observation discouraged him from trying to find out where he was, and to bring attention to his plight. And then there was Ken: the first night after they arrived at the cabin, Ken sodomized Steven; when Steven cried and tried to resist, Ken told him that if he didn't submit, Ken would kill him and bury him so he would never be found.

Later—much later—questions were raised about Steven's apparent docility when taken from his former life. Why didn't Steven simply run away from his abductors? Why didn't he try to get help, by all later accounts, only a few hundred yards away at Yosemite Lodge?

While these might seem outwardly reasonable questions in hindsight, they ignore the central fact of the relationship between an older man and his child-victim. At that point, Ken held complete power over Steven: led to believe that his parents didn't want him and that they had approved Ken's actions, assuaged by Ken's occasional kindness, cowed by the threats to kill him if he didn't cooperate, rendered guilty and ashamed by Ken's sexual assault, lost, uncertain of his place in the world, even of his own family, confused by the rapidly unfolding events, Steven was essentially brainwashed. Slowly, Steven came to understand that whatever happened, his own fate was bound irrevocably to the man who would now claim to be his new father, the man who called himself Ken.

Based on later events, it's also reasonable to assume that Ken dosed his newfound ward with soporifics such as sleeping pills, leaving Steven lethargic and confused during these first few critical weeks.

Ken was hard for Steven to figure out. Just when he

decided that Ken was mean, Ken would surprise him with affection or approval. Ken gave Steven a little dog; Steve named the dog Queenie, and the dog became his best friend.

The week's cold front, the snow, and the advent of the Christmas holidays kept visitors to the park at a minimum in the two or three weeks Steven was at the cabin; even if Steven had been fully aware of his surroundings, there were other events afoot in Yosemite that conspired to draw attention away from Ken, his small friend, and the sudden arrival of Ken's new "son." Many of the park's rangers, in fact, were busy trying to locate the remains of a couple who had just committed suicide by jumping over Yosemite Falls. Having left their clothes and identification at the top of the falls, a man and a woman had leapt into Yosemite Creek, been swept down the stream to a 1,400-foot freefall, and ended by smashing into a built-up cone of rock-hard ice below the falls. Most of the man's shattered body had been recovered; all that was found of the woman was a portion of leg, and it was decided to wait until spring to look for the remainder of the corpse. Truly, the park could be an unforgiving place.

Shortly after Christmas, Ken apparently decided it was time to move on. He quit his job as a bookkeeper at Yosemite Lodge and packed his new "son" and his "son's" little dog into the van, and drove out of the park for the last time. He also told Steven that he now had a new name: from now on, he was Dennis—Dennis Parnell—and Ken was to be "Dennis's" father, Ken

Parnell. "Dennis" was to make sure to call Ken "Dad" from this day forward.

Over the next few years Ken and "Dennis" wandered around northern California, traveling from town to town as Ken looked for work, usually odd jobs. Slowly "Dennis" adjusted to the nomadic lifestyle, and in time came to see Ken as "Dad," just as Ken demanded. The life he'd had in Merced before December 4 began to grow dim; the true reality was the gray van, Queenie, and "Dad," along with the regular sexual assaults, which "Dennis" eventually came to see as something that came with the territory of living with "Dad."

The towns came and went as "Dennis" grew older: first Santa Rosa, but that was too crowded for Ken, so they moved farther up north to Ukiah; from Ukiah, to the small north coast town of Noyo, where Ken took up with a woman named Barbara and her small son, about five years old. Together the four lived in a converted bus, with Barbara selling Bibles to make ends meet.

Throughout this time, Ken enrolled "Dennis" in local schools; to all outward appearances, "Dennis" was what he seemed—the son of Ken, a single father; indeed, there was nothing in either the boy's or the man's behaviors to indicate that anything was other than normal. In fact, Ken joined both the local Eagles lodge and the Grange, and ran the Eagles' weekend flea market; Ken also tended the bar at the lodge, at least until the state's Alcoholic Beverage Commission wanted his fingerprints; that was when Ken decided he was too busy to work the bar anymore.

By the time five years had passed, "Dennis" had become nearly accustomed to his relationship with his "dad"; whatever memories he retained from his former life in Merced were hazy, almost dreamlike. He knew his real name was Steven, but he also knew that his real last name of Stayner was somehow a threat to "Dad," and by extention, himself; at some deep psychological level, "Dennis" knew that whatever happened, he and "Dad" were bound together, and that if something bad happened to "Dad," something bad would also happen to him. So "Dennis" kept his "dad's" secret, and kept to himself.

And it wasn't as if Ken was mean to his "son;" indeed, he was generous, even caring, and often indulgent. Ken gave "Dennis" wide latitude, sometimes even more than "Dennis" thought proper. By the time he was 12, "Dennis" was allowed to smoke and drink and keep his own hours; it was as if "Dad" trusted his "son" completely, so inextricably was the pair bound up in their shared secret.

Eventually, Ken and "Dennis" had to leave the converted bus shared with Barbara when someone pointed out that the storage of fuel containers on the outside of the bus constituted a fire hazard. The landlord who had rented them the space told them they would have to move on. Barbara and her child went their way, and Ken and "Dennis" went theirs. Eventually Ken and "Dennis" moved to a one-room, unelectrified cabin on a ranch near Manchester, California, on the north coast,

not far from Point Arena. "Dennis" attended Point
Arena High School nearby, and Ken got a job in Ukiah,
working as a night bookkeeper at Ukiah's largest hotel,
the Palace. While Ken slept, "Dennis" went to school
every day, smoked when he wanted to, drank when he
wanted to, got into occasional fights at school, a few
scrapes with the law over petty vandalism, and generally kept to himself in the small cabin, seeing "Dad"
every afternoon just before Ken left for work in Ukiah.
It wasn't much of a life, but it was pretty much everything "Dennis" knew, except that his real name was
Steven, and that he and "Dad" shared a terrible secret,
one that he couldn't share with anyone, and especially
not the police.

UKIAH, CALIFORNIA
DECEMBER, 1980

THREE

IT WAS VALENTINE'S DAY. "Dennis"/Steven was 14 years old; half of his life had been spent with Ken Parnell, his "dad." Indeed, life with Ken, hardscrabble and as hand-to-mouth as it was, was normal; it was as if that other life, so many years ago in the barely remembered town of Merced, had only been a dream.

For some time, Ken had been thinking about adding to his "family." Now 48, on at least two occasions Ken had taken "Dennis" with him to Santa Rosa to scout for a potential new "son." On both occasions, "Dennis," troubled by "Dad's" intentions, had contrived to distract or otherwise interfere with Ken's plans to acquire a new "donation." Eventually Ken decided it was too expensive to keep driving to Santa Rosa. He began to look for a possible "son" a little closer to home, in this case, Ukiah, where he normally worked the night shift at the Palace Hotel.

So, too, had Ken decided that "Dennis" couldn't be

relied upon to help entice another addition to his "family." "Dennis's" heart wasn't in it, Ken apparently decided; he began grooming another teenager, a Ukiah high school student, to help him in his quest.

On the rainy afternoon of February 14, 1980, five-year-old Timmy White was walking from his kindergarten class at Ukiah's Yokayo Elementary School to his sitter's house three blocks away. A gray van pulled up to the side of the street, and a young man wearing running shoes and a baseball cap got out and pulled him into the vehicle. An older man was behind the wheel, Timmy saw.

After forcing a dose of sleeping pills down Timmy's throat, the man behind the wheel began to drive, Timmy was to recall later; at some point the van stopped and the other man, the young one with the baseball cap, got out. The next thing Timmy knew, the van was pulling up to a school, and another person got into the van—"Dennis." "Dennis" seemed surprised to find him in the van, Timmy thought. The van drove on, eventually coming to a small, isolated cabin on a ranch in the foothills. Timmy was drowsy, but he noticed that the place seemed surrounded by untended pigs.

Just as happened more than seven years earlier in Merced, the small Ukiah Police Department turned out en masse to search for Timmy shortly after his disappearance, often working double shifts in searching for evidence of his whereabouts. Just like their Merced counterparts in 1972, the 22-member Ukiah department canvassed every house on Timmy's presumed route to his sitter's, scoured storm drains and abandoned re-

frigerators, summoned helicopters for aerial surveil-
lance and canine units for a trace of his scent. One of
Timmy's kindergarten playmates was hypnotized, as
was her mother; lie detector tests were given to
Timmy's mother, stepfather, and babysitter—all to no
avail. It was as if Timmy had simply disappeared from
the face of the earth.

The search for Timmy was compounded by a
drenching rain that began around Valentine's Day and
was to last for nearly two weeks.

For the next two weeks, as police 40 miles away
searched vainly, "Dennis" kept Timmy company, reading him comic books and playing with him; Timmy
begged "Dennis" to help him get away from Ken, at
least when Ken wasn't around; by this time Ken had
cut Timmy's blond hair and dyed it brown. But that
wasn't all that had changed in Ken's little self-created
"family."

As the first week unfolded after Timmy's kidnapping, the bonds of secrecy that for so long had locked
Steven/"Dennis" into the conspiracy with Ken began to
fray. Until Timmy's arrival, it had been just Ken and
"Dennis," joined together for good or bad; each had
secrets on the other, and that tended to keep their worst
sides in check. Steven/"Dennis" had somehow over the
years adjusted to this situation, and indeed, didn't even
really dislike Ken. But seeing Timmy's misery at being
removed from his own real family awoke long-dormant
feelings inside Steven. He could see the pain the sep-
aration was causing Timmy, and was reminded of how

he himself had felt half a lifetime before. And Steven knew it was just a matter a time before Ken would decide to assault Timmy, just as he had Steven years before.

In the dark of the night, while Ken was working at the Palace Hotel, Steven agreed to help Timmy escape. Together they would hitchhike to Ukiah, so Timmy could get home. Steven realized he didn't want what had happened to him to happen to Timmy. But first they had to wait for the rain to stop; in the meantime, they would just have to pretend to Ken that everything was "normal."

Twice the pair set out to make the trip to Ukiah; each time the rains proved too heavy, and they had to turn back. On the third try, after having been passed by several cars, Steven told Timmy they would try one more car, and if they didn't get a ride, they'd go back to the cabin. A pickup truck pulled over. The boys got in, and got a ride all the way into Ukiah.

On March 1, a few hours before midnight, the night officer sitting in the Ukiah Police Department looked up through the glass front door and saw a small boy peering in. At first Officer Robert Warner didn't recognize Timmy as the child the entire department had been searching for for almost two weeks. When Warner got up to move to the door to let the waif in, Timmy ran away.

Warner saw the boy run down the street to a corner, where another, older youth was standing, watching.

Warner alerted a patrol unit, and a few minutes later, both boys were inside the police station.

After officers calmed Timmy down, Timmy was able to say who he was, and the Ukiah authorities realized that the object of their intensive search had found *them*, rather than the other way around. A call was made to Timmy's mother and stepfather, who came immediately to the police station; at first Timmy's mom didn't recognize him through a window, because he was wearing different clothes and his hair was a different color.

"It's not him!" said Timmy's mother.

"Look closer," the police suggested. And at that point, Timmy's parents realized that their son was back from a two-week trip to nowhere. All doubt was erased as soon as Timmy was allowed to see his parents.

That left the question of the older boy, and if the Ukiah police were amazed at Timmy's return, they hadn't heard anything yet.

Shortly after midnight on March 2, the Merced Police Department's Bill Bailey, the lead investigator of the little city's detectives' unit, received a call from the Ukiah police.

They had, the Ukiah officers said, a boy in custody who just might be a Merced missing person named "Steven." Did that ring any bells?

After seven years and an investigative file that now ran to nearly 20 loose-leaf notebooks, the name "Steven" was all-too-familiar to Bailey. But on the other hand, he'd had so many false leads over the previous years, this was just as likely to be another false trail as any other. Still, there were enough similarities in the Ukiah case to warrant sending someone to check it out. Bailey roused detectives Pat Lunney and Jerry Price from their beds in the middle of the night and sent them off to Ukiah, nearly four hours away by car, to see what was what. Both Lunney and Price had long ago concluded that Steven Sayner had to be dead; the return of a kidnap victim seven years later was unheard of by anyone in law enforcement.

About ten in the morning, Sergeant Lunney called Bailey, who by now was a lieutenant.

"Lieutenant," Lunney said, "you won't believe it."

"What?" Bailey said.

"It's him. It's Stayner," Lunney told Bailey. "He looks just like the kid on the flyer seven years ago." Not only did Steven look like the boy who had been missing for seven years, he remembered his street, his real mother and father, even his second-grade teacher. After half a lifetime among the missing, Steven Stayner would get a chance to go home again.

FOUR

IT WASN'T QUITE THAT SIMPLE, OF course. For one thing, even before they knew about Merced, the Ukiah police had a lot of questions for Steven/"Dennis." Just how had he met up with little Timmy White, anyway?

Steven still had loyalty to Ken. While he didn't want Timmy to go through the same fate he himself had suffered, he didn't want to get "Dad" into trouble, either. After all, Ken was the only Dad he had, at that point. And Steven still remembered what Ken had told him: that his own mother and father didn't want him, they couldn't afford him, that they'd given him to Ken for Ken to take care of him, and that Ken had legally adopted him. Ken had been good to him for the most part, Steven thought. He'd done what was right in returning Timmy; now the cops should just let him go, no questions asked.

But the Ukiah police weren't quite so willing to let bygones be bygones—and little Timmy helped shed some light on good old "Dad." They'd been living in a one-room cabin over by the ocean, Timmy said; there was no electricity and there were lots of pigs around. Every night "Dad" disappeared, and "Dennis" had taken care of him, Timmy explained. They'd decided to try to get to Ukiah more than a week before, but it had been raining too heavily.

Steven continued to remain defensive about Ken's real identity, or where he could be found. Ukiah Police Chief David Johnson came in and pressed the questioning.

"He fairly reluctantly gave the name to me," Johnson said later. "You could tell he thought this man was his father. He was visibly shaken that his father was going to get into trouble. He wasn't sure if he wanted to go back to Merced."

But once Steven had given Ken's name and the fact that he worked as the night bookkeeper at Ukiah's Palace Hotel, it was only a few minutes before "Dad" was behind bars.

As for Steven, detectives Lunney and Price found themselves trying to convince the 14-year-old that his real mother and father really did love him and wanted him back. On Sunday afternoon, the detectives and Steven drove back to Merced, where nearly 500 friends and family members gathered at the Stayner house to welcome him home. One who came to the miraculous reunion was Steve's older brother Cary, then 18. Cary had been on his way back from a camping trip to Yosemite Park when he heard the news broadcast on his car radio.

"I almost drove off the road," Cary was to say later, so unexpected was the news.

Steven's return from the missing after seven years, coupled with the rescue of Timmy White—combined with the saga of their hitchhiking 40 miles through the rain and mud for help—ignited a news media firestorm in northern California. Within hours, news crews from radio, television, and newspapers were on their way to Ukiah and Merced alike, agog at the sensational nature of a story with what appeared to be two happy endings. This was the kind of thing people loved to read about and watch on television, and the media pulled out all the stops, day after day.

At a press conference in Ukiah, Timmy White told his story, and described how Steven had kept him company by playing with him and reading comic books to him, and how the two had decided to try to get to Ukiah on their own. Ken—whom Timmy knew only as "the man"—had treated him well enough, Timmy said, except for one occasion when he was spanked. But overall, Timmy said, the experience was sort of an adventure.

In Merced, a huge crowd of reporters camped out in the Stayners' front yard, waiting for Steven to make an appearance; the crowd intimidated Queenie the dog, who wasn't used to so many people. Sergeant Lunney helped guide Steven through the media's questions.

After describing the events of his abduction seven years earlier, Steven said, he came to see his kidnapper as his father. It was only when Timmy was taken that

Steve began to think about doing something desperate to get away from Ken.

"I got to like Timmy," Steven said. "I didn't want the same thing that happened to me to happen to Timmy."

Asked how he felt about Ken, Steven said his fake "dad" had treated him well, and that he felt sorry for him; even so, he said, he didn't want to see him again.

Reporters repeatedly asked Steven why he didn't try to run away during the seven years, but Lunney wouldn't let him answer. In fact, at least twice over the years Steven had tried to call his parents; on the first time he couldn't remember the number, and on a second try, an operator was unable to find the number for him. On another occasion, while living in Santa Rosa, Steven had run away, but got lost in the dark; since he was more afraid of the dark than he was of Ken, he returned to Ken's trailer.

When he was asked how it felt to be "home," Steven appeared both shy and nervous. Although he'd tried to remember as much as he could about his former life, it was clear that over the years everyone and everything had "changed quite a bit."

That, of course, was an understatement of the first magnitude. When Steven had first been taken, he was seven years old, a little boy. The Steven who was returned to his family was a 14-year-old man-child, half-wild in some ways, used to taking care of himself and doing whatever he wanted to do, including smoking, drinking, cussing, and getting into the occasional fight. That expectations were oceans apart for both Steven and his family was only to be expected; Kay Stayner, in fact, had saved Steven's Christmas presents from 1972. In her mind, her son was still a little boy, just one grown suddenly large.

This wasn't going to be easy. For the better part of a decade Steven had been frozen in the Stayner family's mind's eye as a second-grader; now to find him nearly fully formed and fairly headstrong was a shock. Living with an absent ghost was one thing, especially when no adjustment was required to a mere memory; integrating a back-to-life legend into a family that had made their silent accommodations with one another years before was another matter entirely.

It helped not at all that the circumstances of Steven's return made him something of a celebrity. Indeed, the merchants and townspeople of Ukiah had decided to present Steven with a $15,000 reward for the return of Timmy White. When reporters asked Steven what he would do with the money, Steven said he wanted to buy a motorcycle.

Someone decided that the best thing that could happen was to make Steven's new environment as normal as possible. That meant enrolling Steven at Merced High School for classes, which itself created another media frenzy.

As Steven arrived for his first day of school, a television news crew camped out in front of the school to record his arrival. Joseph Reeves, the principal, wasn't happy. It was going to be hard enough for Steven Stayner to return to normalcy without his every movement being recorded for the evening news.

"There's a bit of a mob scene here," Reeves said, "but we're hoping that the novelty will wear off. He has a tough row to hoe, but we'll do everything we can to keep his head above water."

As it turned out, Reeves's prediction was, if anything, woefully understated.

Steven Stayner didn't just have a row to hoe, he had a mountain. Not the least of his problems were his fellow students at the new high school: not only was he a celebrity, there were all the snide remarks. Why hadn't Steven run away from his kidnapper? What sort of things did Steven do for the man—*you know?* There were cruel jokes, harassment, a few fights. Mostly, Steven was looked upon as some sort of freak, and at an age when being different can be one of the most difficult of experiences. Lying beneath the teenage tormenting was the thinly hidden strand of homophobia— he must be one of *them*; why else would he have stayed around so long?

And if there were troubles at school, it was even harder at home.

"That family was absolutely devastated," one former Merced police official recalled years later. "They were just destroyed—first by the kidnapping, then again when he came back. You just can't expect everything to pick up the way things were; everything's different."

Different, for example, in Steven's relationship with his mother Kay. Always the strong one of the family, Kay now had to cope with a willful teenager, while in her mind's eye she kept seeing Steven as he was when he disappeared at seven years of age. There was a near-constant jarring of expectations and adjustments on both sides, as Steven learned to know his mother again, and Kay learned that the Steven who had come home was not at all like the little boy who had been taken.

And Del. For years the stealing of his son had seared his soul, had saddened him with a grief that could barely be expressed. Until finally Del had decided to cover that hole up, to bind over that wound by giving his son up for lost. Now here he was back, not much at all like Del or the other children, a half-man, half-child whose behavior often seemed inexplicable. The man who had stolen Steven Stayner had taken more than a boy, he had taken the heart out of an entire family.

And there were Steven's brothers and sisters: for seven years he had been the secret center of their pain, the mysterious vacuum that sucked all their emotions into an insatiable void, the proximate cause of their parents' inconsolable sadness; that had been a given for almost as long as they could remember. And now suddenly that larger-than-life hole was filled, packed with some real person, also larger-than-life, but inevitably alien. Who was this brother they had mourned, but now had come back among them, so different, and yet the center of all the attention?

It was all very confusing, for everyone; and of all the difficult adjustments that had to be made, probably the hardest was thrust upon Steven. Within a few years of his return, Steven had moved out to live on his own. Coming home was much easier said than accomplished, as it turned out.

FIVE

ALL THOSE ADJUSTMENTS STILL lay in the future, however, as the news media's focus on the Steven Stayner story turned on the man who had claimed to be "Dennis's" father for so many years, Ken Parnell.

People in Ukiah and Noyo who had known Ken Parnell for the previous five or six years were shocked to discover that not only was he *not* "Dennis's" father, he was a suspected kidnapper and child molester. He just didn't seem the type, nearly everyone agreed. Even the Mendocino County District Attorney Joe Allen—who would have to prosecute Parnell for kidnapping Timmy White—tended to see the situation rather more benignly than circumstances seemed to warrant.

"It seems he wanted to build a family for himself without going to the trouble of getting married," Allen told reporters the day after Parnell's arrest at the Palace Hotel.

This was, indeed, putting a charitable interpretation

on Ken's actions over the past seven years: making it seem as though Ken's only real sin was that he loved children as much as any man.

That Parnell loved them differently, however, quickly became apparent when police and reporters began delving into Ken's background.

If anything, Ken Parnell had had an even harder life than Steven Stayner, it soon became apparent; indeed, in one way, Parnell's predilection for stealing children and "adopting" them was a clear manifestation of his own inner yearning for normalcy—a normalcy that could never be possible given Parnell's own upbringing.

Born in the Depression year of 1931 in west Texas near Amarillo, Parnell was the only son of a man who had deserted his family when Parnell was five years old. Two years later, Parnell's mother took her seven-year-old son to Bakersfield, California, where mother and son lived in poverty, and Kenneth Parnell began embarking on a series of self-destructive acts.

At the age of eight, Ken focused a bright beam of light into his eyes for so long his vision was damaged; a few years later he attempted to pull all his teeth out, and on several other occasions he attempted to commit suicide.

At the age of 13, in the middle of World War II, Ken was lured into a car by an older man and sexually assaulted.

As the war wound to a close, Parnell began a series of homosexual affairs with older men, and got into re-

peated trouble with the law by setting fires and stealing
cars.

In retrospect, Parnell's actions seem to have fit a
classic pattern: deprived of his own father, and feeling
worthless, Parnell got the attention he craved from male
authority figures by acting either badly or seductively.
The principles of juvenile psychology and the principles of child development then being in their infancy,
the system reacted to Parnell the way it did with most
"bad" kids from poor homes: branded an incorrigible
and a mental misfit, Parnell was institutionalized.

A psychiatrist, Dr. Richard D. Loewenberg, who began treating Parnell in his mid-teens, noted that Parnell
had developed "a peculiar tendency to search for trouble and punishment."

Doubtless at least some of this "peculiar tendency"
related to Parnell's often tempestuous relationship with
his mother; Loewenberg came to conclude that if Ken's
mother's fondest wish were granted, her troubled son
would simply run away, never to be seen again.

It was perhaps with that goal in mind that Ken, at
18, married a Bakersfield girl he had met in high
school. The young couple had a daughter, but the marriage soon foundered.

Driven by desires he had trouble understanding, in
March of 1951, Parnell kidnapped an eight-year-old
Bakersfield boy by pretending to be a police officer,
drove him to an arroyo outside of town, sexually assaulted him, and then drove him back to town. Parnell
later admitted that he thought of killing the boy to conceal his crime, but then thought better of it. Bakersfield

police had little difficulty identifying Parnell, and Ken was arrested. Loewenberg, in an assessment for the court, termed Parnell a "sexual psychopath," as did two other doctors retained by the court.

Quickly convicted, Parnell's marriage to his high school girlfriend disintegrated, and Parnell was sent to San Quentin State Prison for a four-year term. Released for the first time in 1955, Parnell violated his parole, and was returned to San Quentin for another year before earning a second release in 1956.

Parnell next wandered to Utah, where, in 1960 he was arrested for holding up a gas station three blocks from the Mormon Tabernacle in Salt Lake City. Convicted again, Parnell was sentenced to five-years-to-life at the Utah State Prison in Draper, Utah.

In 1967, Parnell was released on parole, with the proviso that he leave the state of Utah within 48 hours and never return.

This skeletal outline of Kenneth Parnell's background, however, leaves out some of the most important aspects of his personality: Parnell was peculiarly gifted with the inborn talent of most psychopaths to seem what others wanted to see in him; he was at his best with children and less intelligent adults, who trusted him as a steady, seemingly kind, reasonable, and mature adult. In fact, Parnell, like many psychopathic personalities, was an adroit manipulator of others.

This talent in part accounted for Parnell's success in convincing a diminutive little night janitor employed at

Yosemite Lodge to help him entice Steven Stayner into the van in Merced back in 1972.

This was the "little man" Steven recalled, who had asked him if his family wanted to make a donation. Under questioning from Lunney and Price, Steven was able to remember that the little man was barely five feet tall, smoked heavily, and that he worked as a janitor at the lodge. Using an array of lodge employee photos, Steven was able to pick the janitor as Ken's accomplice without hesitation.

Price and Lunney went to Yosemite, where they arrested the man without incident. The janitor expressed relief that he'd finally been caught; in fact, helping Parnell kidnap Steven Stayner was the only crime he'd ever committed in his life, and it had preyed on his conscience for seven years.

"Thank God it's over," the janitor told Lunney and Price. "I'm really glad that kid is safe." He hadn't talked to Parnell since 1973, when Parnell wanted money, he said, and he'd had no idea where Parnell had been for the past seven years.

Still, it was clear that Parnell was something more than the garden variety sexual psychopath; after all, it is the rarest of child molesters who want their victims to call them "dad." Here, in fact, is a clue to the inner workings of Parnell's twisted mind: while he craved the sexual relationship he forced upon his victims, that wasn't all. What Parnell also wanted was something he'd never had for himself: a father, a role model, a family; and if he had to steal children to create this image in his own mind, the roots of his pathology were at least explicable, if unforgiveable. In Steven Stayner, Kenneth Parnell had for seven years something he'd always yearned for: a family, an ongoing relationship in which he was the head, a relationship he could control and take the inner and outer satisfaction in, to help him play the role he'd never had in his own life: "Dad." It was only when Steven Stayner began to grow up that "Dad" decided he needed a new son.

INTERLUDE,
1980–1989

SIX

WITHIN A FEW WEEKS OF THEIR AR-
rest, Parnell and Murphy were charged in connection
with the kidnappings of Steven Stayner and Timmy
White. Because the crimes occurred in different counties, there would be two different trials, Parnell for
Timmy's kidnapping in Mendocino County, and Parnell and Murphy for Steven's kidnapping in Merced
County.

After preliminary hearings on both cases in both
counties, defense lawyers for both men asked that the
trials be moved from each county; the pre-trial publicity in both Ukiah and Merced was too intense for either
man to receive a fair trial. Eventually both cases were
transferred to Alameda County, in Oakland, California.

Nearly two years after Steven and Timmy walked
through the rain to Ukiah, Parnell was found guilty of
kidnapping and conspiracy in the abduction of Steven
Stayner; that followed by several months his earlier
conviction for kidnapping Timmy White. Steven Stay-

ner was the star witness against both Parnell and Murphy, as Timmy was against Parnell in the Ukiah case.

Parnell was sentenced to serve up to seven years for kidnapping Timmy, but because of a quirk in the state's sentencing law, he could only get 20 additional months for the kidnapping of Steven. The quirk meant that Murphy, who was consistently portrayed by both prosecutors and his defense lawyers as Parnell's dupe, would have to serve a longer sentence than Parnell for Steven's kidnapping. In all, the way things would work out, Parnell would serve fewer years in prison for his crimes than Steven had spent as Parnell's "son."

As for Steven Stayner, his short-lived reunion with his family soon metamorphosed into a more arm's length relationship. It simply wasn't possible for him to return home as if nothing had happened. School became increasingly difficult for him; occasionally, Merced Police Sergeant Jerry Price would run into Steve around town, and while on the surface things seemed fine, Price sensed there was a lot going on beneath the surface.

"There were a lot of secrets there," Price recalled later; and why not?

Bit by bit, Steven learned to tune out the past, the way he'd done for so many years when he was "Dennis." He wrapped himself up in television shows, in books, his motorcycle.

Whatever ambitions Steven might have had as a second-grader were long gone, somehow ground up in the lost years. As the 1980s unfolded, Steve took a job as a pizza deliverer; it was enough to be content. Steve met a girl, and they were married; two small children followed. Still, he had relatively few friends; for that he blamed Parnell.

"I've always shied away from people," Steven told a reporter for the *San Francisco Chronicle* in May of 1989, "because any (male) friend I ever had, Parnell made advances toward."

The occasion of the interview was the imminent broadcast of a made-for-television movie about his kidnapping and escape—"I Know My Name Is Steven," which was to be broadcast that month on NBC.

It had been more than 16 years since the kidnapping, nine since he'd walked to freedom with Timmy White, and yet Steven Stayner was still something of an unwilling celebrity. He had tried to pass the intervening years in obscurity, but the past still came back. Still, Stayner said, he was slowly coming to grips with what the years with Parnell had done to him. For one thing, he said, he learned to erect walls to keep people from getting close to him.

"I was protecting Parnell," Steven told *The Chronicle*'s Torri Minton. "I was protecting myself. I didn't want anybody to know what was going on. I made up excuses why my friends couldn't stay the night with me, why we couldn't do certain things with Parnell, like go camping. It was one lie right after another.

"What I did not want to do was have someone find out that my life was not normal, that it included sexual abuse, which I was trying to hide. To hide that I had to protect Parnell."

Getting out of high school before graduation (he left in his senior year) was a tremendous relief, he said. No one greeted him with the remark, *Oh, you're the one who was . . .* Out of school he was just another person, someone no one knew.

Steven wasn't entirely happy with the way the made-for-television movie portrayed him, he said. Yes, it was true he was rebellious when he first returned home, and had trouble with curfews and other such parental rules; but it wasn't true that he was rude and insulting to Del and Kay. The movie showed him arguing a lot with his parents, but that wasn't really his way; rather than argue, he'd just shut off, the way he did with Parnell.

If anything held promise in his life, Steven added, it was the love of his wife and children, three and two years old. They accepted him for who he was, no questions asked: just a normal dad.

So, a happy ending for Steven Stayner—right?

Tragically, it was not to happen. Less than two months after the movie about his return from oblivion was broadcast, Steven Stayner rode his motorcycle broadside into a car that abruptly turned in front of him. He was killed instantly.

The car's driver was uninsured, and fled the scene— a fatal, senseless, hit-and-run accident that claimed the life of a boy who had only just begun to live.

By that time, the Vietnam war wasn't even a memory for a new generation, Henry Kissinger was in retirement, Richard Nixon was a respected elder statesman, Judge Sirica was dead, the Watergate burglars were either evangelists, trivia questions, or radio hosts, and the best part of nearly a whole decade was a blank to the family of Kay and Del Stayner and their remaining children. Kenneth Parnell had been out of prison for two years.

But the park at Yosemite still beckoned.

EL PORTAL, CALIFORNIA
FEBRUARY, 1999

SEVEN

IT WAS SOMETIME IN THE MIDDLE of the dinner hour, others later thought they remembered. The two teenaged girls were in the restaurant, in the middle of their hamburgers and fries, when an older woman came in and talked briefly, whereupon the trio left the restaurant, but not before the woman paid for the meals with a credit card. Some thought the girls said they would be back to finish their meals, but they didn't return. With that last, all-too-ordinary act, Carole Sund, 42, her daughter Juliana, 15, and family friend Silvina Pelosso, 16, simply vanished.

At first, no one noticed. The dishes were cleared away, and no one thought much about the sudden departure. The following day, Tuesday, February 16, 1999, the motel room that had been rented by the mother, daughter, and their friend was found unoccupied, damp towels in the bathroom, the room key in plain view. All the luggage was gone. It was assumed that the two Sunds and Ms. Pelosso had simply gotten an early start.

Late that same evening, Carole Sund's husband, Jens, 43, and their three other children arrived at San Francisco International Airport, where they had planned to meet Carole, Juli, and Silvina and all fly to Arizona to visit Jens Sund's sister before a planned excursion to the Grand Canyon. The flight from the Sunds' hometown of Eureka, California, was very late, and when the trio didn't show up, Jens concluded that either Carole and the girls had taken an earlier flight, or that for some reason they had been temporarily delayed.

Jens Sund wasn't particularly worried about the mix-up. His wife was a confident, self-reliant woman, capable of taking care of herself in almost any situation. A businesswoman and an inveterate community activist in Eureka, Carole Sund was a superb, even obsessive, organizer and planner. If anyone had fouled up, Jens thought, it was probably him. Maybe he'd taken the wrong flight, and Carole and the girls had already gone ahead.

Jens and the three other children boarded their own flight to Phoenix, expecting to see Carole and the girls waiting for them when they arrived.

It didn't occur to Jens to check at the car rental counter to see whether Carole had returned the red, 1999 Pontiac Grand Prix she had rented the previous Saturday at the airport for the trip to Stockton and Yosemite. If he had, he would have learned some disquieting news: the car had not yet been returned.

As he and his children, Jonah, 14, Gina, 13, and Jimmy, 10, flew through the dark night toward Phoenix, Jens Sund remained unworried about his wife. Carole was so organized, so capable of handling almost any situation it was unthinkable that anything might happen that would be beyond her control.

"She's a fighter," Jens said later, and so was Juli. The idea that someone might attack Carole and get away with it seemed scarcely credible to Jens.

He had first met Carole when they were both in high school in Santa Rosa, California. Jens was the son of an El Salvadoran mother and a Danish father, and was fluent in both Spanish and English. When Jens's father died at an early age, both Jens and his brother Ken, had to help support their family. Carole, in contrast, was the daughter of Francis and Carole Carrington, fourth generation descendants of one of northern California's wealthiest families, whose roots in the area went back to the late nineteenth century.

As a high school girl, Carole was fortunate enough to spend about six months as a foreign exchange student in Argentina, where she stayed with the family of Raquel Cucco in a village called Las Varillas. Although Raquel was a year older than Carole and a college student, the two young women became fast friends. As Carole prepared to return to Santa Rosa, she and Raquel traded gold rings, and promised to continue their friendship for the rest of their lives.

After Carole graduated with a business degree from San Francisco State University, she and Jens were married in 1978; they honeymooned at Yosemite National Park.

In 1983, with Jens running his own paint contracting business, and Carole working in the Carrington family business, Carole gave birth to Juliana. Two years later, the Sunds and their baby daughter visited Raquel and her husband, Jose Pelosso, and the Pelossos' three-year-old daughter, Silvina, in Argentina for two months. Carole gave her ring back to Raquel Pelosso in demonstration of their friendship, and Raquel promised to visit Carole and Jens sometime in the future, when she would return the gesture.

Instead, it was Silvina who was the first of the Pelossos to make the trip to the United States. Silvina arrived in Eureka to stay with the Sunds in late November, 1998, and would stay with the Sund family until February 12, when she, Carole Sund, and Juli would embark on their fateful trip to Yosemite. Silvina had been scheduled to return to Argentina in early March of 1999.

Now, as Jens Sund and his three younger children arrived at his sister's house in Phoenix, there was no sign of Carole, Juli, or Silvina. Still Jens remained unconcerned; surely there would be some simple explanation for the mix-up, even though it was entirely uncharacteristic behavior of the detail-oriented, highly organized Carole.

By the following morning, Jens was still not particularly worried; he played a round of golf. It was only after the round was over, and no one had yet heard from Carole, that Jens began to wonder whether something bad had happened to his wife, his oldest daughter, and their young friend from Argentina.

Jens started making telephone calls. One went to the Carringtons back in California; no, Francis and Carole said, they hadn't heard from their daughter. Jens next called the California Highway Patrol, and asked whether any report had been made on his wife or the rental car. When it appeared that no such report had been made, Jens put a call to the Mariposa County Sheriff's Department, and told deputies there that his wife, daughter, and their friend were apparently missing.

At that point, Jens hopped a plane back to San Francisco, en route to Mariposa, California. The search for Carole Sund, Juli Sund, and Silvina Pelosso was about to get under way.

The small town of Mariposa, about 1,800 souls and a little over three square miles in size, stands athwart one of the major roads into Yosemite Park, Highway 140; in any given year, as many as 1.4 million people a year will drive through the village on the way over the hill to Merced Canyon and ultimately El Portal and Yosemite. As a result, the small town that was once the center of some of the earliest gold-bearing quartz mines in the Sierra Nevada is now almost entirely dependent on mining the tourists, renting motel rooms, serving meals, and outfitting weeklong trekkers and Winnebago enthusiasts alike for their forays into the sprawling park.

Aside from its California Mining and Mineral Museum, probably the most impressive building in Mariposa is the Mariposa County Courthouse, a white, two-story structure first erected in 1854, which Mariposans claim to be the oldest public building continually occupied in the state. There was a time when the offices of the county sheriff were housed in the courthouse, but those days are long gone; today, the Mariposa Sheriff's Department occupies two buildings just up a slight hill from the historic courthouse, amid the full range of modern communications and vehicular equipment necessary to patrol nearly 14,450 square miles, most of it up and down, and keep the peace among the county's 16,000 permanent residents, to say nothing of the vacationing hordes.

The man in charge of the Mariposa Sheriff's Department, Sheriff C. A. "Pelk" Edwards, had less than three dozen deputies to cover some of the most difficult terrain in California, a landscape bound together by meandering, often substandard roads of mud and gravel that wound around peaks, down into inpenetrable canyons, and over trackless expanses of sage, Ponderosa pine, and cedar trees—beautiful to behold from a distance, but deadly for those who might become lost in its vastness.

Away from the park itself and off the major roads, there was another, hidden Mariposa County: with its isolation and the live-and-let-live attitude of its permanent residents, the county was a stange mix of the retired well-to-do, the professional classes who served the park, and a sizeable number of ne'er-do-wells on the lam from other jurisdictions or on probation for various crimes, many of whom were attracted to the

area by the isolation, the freedom, and the regular, if
low-paying, jobs available from servicing the tourist
industry—all in all, a state of affairs that had hardly
changed since the abduction of young Steven Stayner
some 27 years before, when, as we have seen, Kenneth
Parnell had used the park itself and his menial job as
a cover for his crime.

Here was a place to hide out, for those so inclined—
a sort of modern-day hole in the wall where outlaws
could gather without too much scrutiny from the police,
where a patch of marijuana could be raised without
undue attention or a methamphetamine lab could be
operated without much concern.

Indeed, many of the foothill counties fronting the
higher peaks of the Sierras could claim much of the
same sort of subclass—a sort of Ozarks of the Pacific—
where the revenuers weren't wanted, and everyone
learned to mind their own business, just as things had
been dating back to Prohibition, when hundreds of stills
making sour mash whiskey dotted the woods. Only the
nature of the chemicals had changed over the years; the
people, living on the edge, had remained the same.

This was the environment that Sheriff Pelk and his
pitifully shorthanded force had to contend with when
Jens Sund reported that his wife, his daughter, and their
friend from Argentina appeared to be missing.

That Carole, Juli, and Silvina couldn't be accounted
for wasn't that unusual, the Mariposa deputies knew.
All too often, relatives called either the Sheriff's Department, or more usually the park itself, to report miss-

ing family members, only to see the family members
turn up elsewhere because of unforeseen circumstances:
a car breakdown, a last-minute impulse to see something else in the park, even a decision to simply not
come home for a while, often for personal reasons.

The deputies collected the information from Jens,
and took the first, routine step to determining the
whereabouts of Carole, Juli, and Silvina: they called
the El Portal motel the women had been registered at
the night before: Cedar Lodge, a sprawling, 206-room
facility on Highway 140 about eight miles from the
park's entrance. Jens told the deputies that he had
talked to Carole the night of Monday, February 15,
while the women were still at Cedar Lodge; she'd mentioned nothing unusual, and as far as Jens could tell,
the trio were still adhering to the itinerary that Carole
had mapped out before they'd left Eureka on February
12.

But, Jens continued, that was the thing: Carole was
so meticulous in making plans and following them that
it was inconceivable that she would alter her plans in
almost any case, and certainly not without notifying the
rest of the family. Carole was so organized, Jens said,
she mapped out her trips in precise detail with a computer program, right down to mileage and estimated
times of arrival and scheduled departures; to Carole,
the idea of skylarking off on an unplanned jaunt was
nearly unthinkable.

The Mariposa authorities checked with the Cedar
Lodge management, and learned that the trio had apparently left the lodge early on the morning of February

16; damp towels in the bathroom seemed to indicate that at least one person had taken a shower. The key had been left in the room, and there were no signs of anything left behind. The beds appeared to have been made.

Further checking showed that the three had been seen in the restaurant sometime between 6:30 and 7:30 P.M., and that a video and VCR had been rented Monday evening. Because the motel was less than full, no one had yet bothered to clean it up. A motel employee had been in the room Wednesday morning to retrieve the VCR the trio had rented for their movies, and nothing seemed out of the ordinary then. Beyond that, no one seemed to know what had happened to Carole, Juli, and Silvina, not even where they were headed next.

Jens Sund knew the answer to that one: according to Carole's written itinerary, the trio had intended to drive to Stockton on Tuesday, February 16, to take a tour of the University of the Pacific campus with some friends before continuing on to San Francisco to meet Jens and the other children. But Jens had learned that they never showed up at UOP. Originally, the trio had planned to fly to Modesto from San Francisco; when their flight was delayed, they decided to rent the car instead. They still had Tuesday night reservations for a flight from Modesto to San Francisco, where they were to have met Jens, but had failed to arrive. Jens didn't know whether Carole planned to return the rented car at Modesto or San Francisco; what did seem apparent was that Carole, Juli, and Silvina had disappeared

sometime between Monday night and Tuesday afternoon at the latest.

While all of this sounded a bit peculiar to the Mariposa authorities, it wasn't all that unusual. Sometimes
people changed their plans; with 4 million people a
year streaming through the park, it was foolhardy to
jump to any conclusions, especially when it came to
ordinary human behavior.

The next step was to put out the word to the authorities in the park, the law enforcement contingent of
the park's rangers. Patrolling in four-wheel-drive vehicles, it was the rangers' job to keep order among the
hordes of visitors who streamed in and out of the park
on a daily basis. Rangers were asked to keep an eye
out for the red Pontiac Carole had rented in San Francisco. Meanwhile, the California Highway Patrol was
asked to keep watch for the car on the roads leading
from Yosemite to Stockton and to San Francisco. There
matters rested throughout much of Thursday, February
18; it was as if the earth had swallowed Carole, Juli,
and Silvina without a trace.

But all this changed the following day, when a teenage girl in Modesto, California, walking across a me-
dian strip near a busy intersection, discovered a wallet
carrying a driver's license and credit cards belonging
to Carole Sund.

EIGHT

Up until this point the Mariposa and park authorities had been operating on either of two assumptions: one, that Carole, Juli, and Silvina had, for some unknown reason voluntarily deviated from their planned intinerary, and would eventually turn up; or, more ominously, that some potentially fatal mishap had occurred, such as a car wreck.

After all, the country leading into and out of Yosemite was quite rugged, with hairpin turns and sharp drop-offs; the weather had been alternately raining and snowing. It was entirely possible that Carole had missed a turn and crashed on her way out of El Portal Tuesday morning; in that case the missing red Pontiac might even then be lying hidden in some easy-to-overlook canyon somewhere off the side of Highway 140, concealed in brush and woods, awaiting a belated discovery.

But the recovery of Carole's wallet—minus cash but loaded with credit cards, well over 100 miles away from Yosemite—suggested at least three other alternatives, each of them even more sinister: either Carole and the girls had made it out of El Portal, had driven to Modesto, where Carole and the girls had met with some sort of foul play, such as a carjacking; or second, that the trio had crashed on the way out, and that someone had come along, looted the wallet, and failed to report the location of the wreck; or third, that the three had been carjacked either in El Portal or the park proper, or even—given the Sund family's wealth—had somehow been kidnapped.

Because the discovery of the wallet seemed to indicate the strong possibility of foul play, either in Mariposa County or Modesto, Modesto authorities decided to call in the Federal Bureau of Investigation for assistance, while in Mariposa County an effort was redoubled to develop credible sightings of the trio after Monday night.

Since his return to California from Arizona the previous Wednesday evening, Jens Sund had several meetings with the Mariposa authorities; then, assisted by other family members and friends, Jens began searching both the park and the Highway 140 corridor, looking for some sign of the red car.

But the Friday discovery of Carole's wallet in Modesto changed everything: now Jens and the rest of his family, including the Carringtons, had to prepare themselves for the possibility that Carole, Juli, and Silvina might have been kidnapped, or worse. The Sunds and Carringtons relocated their own base of operations to

Modesto, and on Sunday, February 23, held a press conference in Modesto: perhaps anticipating or hoping to instigate a ransom demand, the family offered $250,000 for information leading to the safe return of Carole, Juli, and Silvina, no questions asked. Meanwhile, family members, assisted by Modesto police, the park authorities, and Mariposa deputies, began circulating flyers in the park, in El Portal, and in Modesto near where Carole's wallet was found, in the hope that some witness might come forward who could shed light on what had become of the trio.

One thing seemed increasingly clear: the rented red Pontiac almost certainly was no longer in the Yosemite/Mariposa area. Searchers from the Park Service, the Mariposa County Sheriff's Department, and the California Highway Patrol had combed the highways leading into and out of the park both on foot and from the air, and had discovered nothing. If the car were still in the area, said Mariposa Sheriff's Sergeant Doug Binniweis, "we would have located it by now."

Asked if his agency was investigating the disappearances as a simple missing persons case or a kidnapping, Binniweis could only shrug. "Right now," he said, "I don't know."

Making its own appearance at the press conference, a spokesman for the FBI, Nick Rossi, said his agency was treating the matter as a potential kidnapping until information showed otherwise.

As a general rule, law enforcement authorities are of two minds about the posting of rewards: broadly speak-

ing, on one hand a substantial reward is likely to stim-
ulate public attention, and potentially lead to valuable
clues; on the other hand, however, the larger the reward, the larger the number of false leads that may be
turned in, however well-intentioned—and sometimes
not.

In an environment with a sizeable number of
subsistance-level residents, a quarter-million dollar
jackpot can whet the imagination. In this case, with
precious little to go on—three women in a missing red
car—almost any sighting that conformed to the basics
had a chance. The problem for investigators was to
winnow the grains of reality from the dry stalks of in-
spired imagination.

And too, the posting of a large reward has additional
advantages and drawbacks—not least of which is attention from the news media. By the week following
the disappearance, the northern California news media
had recognized the Sund-Pelosso mystery as a surefire
subject of viewer/reader interest, especially with
$250,000 now in the pot. Within hours, representatives
of most of northern California's major media organi-
zations were in Modesto to attend Jens Sund's press
conference; most soon divided their forces between the
motel in Modesto the Sunds/Carringtons adopted as
their headquarters, a nearby hotel adopted by the FBI,
and the Cedar Lodge at El Portal, waiting for some sort
of denouement. Eventually, as the search went on for
more than a month, even the national media dropped
in to see what was going on.

In truth, the disappearance of Carole, Juli, and Silvina had all of what the news media likes to call "the elements" of a good story, and in abundance. Apart from the mystery itself and the reward, there was the very setting: one of America's most famous national parks, with breathtaking scenery for backdrop visuals, the sort of place millions of Americans had been to and could relate to; a wealthy family, essentially saying money was no object as long as the missing could be found safe and sound; the likelihood of foul play, particularly against three unarmed, innocent and defenseless women tourists; a strong Sund family presence in Modesto, making themselves available for anguished interviews in a desperate effort to focus public attention on their plight; and even the possibility of international intrigue: after all, Silvina was from a wealthy Argentinian family, which at least suggested the possibility, however remote, that the disappearance might be connected to political upheavals in that country that were more than 20 years old.

But of all of these, the biggest element was the park itself.

As one of the first two national parks (the other was Yellowstone), Yosemite had a long, colorful and even violent history even before it was designated as a federal park in 1890.

The history of Yosemite as we know it began in the last ice age, when a series of glaciers lay over the crown of uplifted granite that formed the rim of the present-day Sierra Nevada mountains, themselves thrust up over millions of years' pressure from below. As global temperatures slowly warmed, the glacier that would become the Merced River ate through the softer portions of granite atop the Sierra, leaving the harder sections behind in a sort of circular bowl; these would become the towering gray cliff faces so beloved by climbers and photographers today.

After the Merced glacier finally melted, a dam of rock and gravel plugged the western end of the U-shaped valley, leaving a prehistoric lake. Eventually, rock and silt runoff from the towering heights above filled the lake, forming today's valley floor.

Probably the first English-speaking person to visit Yosemite Valley was the mountain man Joe Walker, sometime in 1833, when that curmudgeonly trapper first crossed the Sierras in search of California horses to steal for sale east of the Rocky Mountains. It appears that the Spanish colonists of California at the time had no inkling of Yosemite's existence.

That certainly wasn't true of the native Americans who had lived in California for thousands of years before the Spanish or mountain men like Walker arrived. Indeed, until the discovery of gold in California in 1848, most of the population of California was Native American, and it was their tragic misfortune that a yellow metal worthless to them was instrumental in the destruction of their culture, to say nothing of their very lives. By some estimates, the native population of California declined by as much as *two-thirds* during the California Gold Rush.

The story of Yosemite's "discovery" and naming is best told by writer Rebecca Solnit in the November/

December 1992 issue of *Sierra*, the Sierra Club's publication.

To summarize Solnit's reconstruction, Yosemite itself first came to the outside world's attention in 1851, and it took a bit of ethnic cleansing on the part of the gold-crazed whites to do it. As it happened, another mountain man, one Jim Savage, born in Illinois around 1823, was the responsible party; Savage's own family lore holds that he was kidnapped by Indians as an adolescent, or perhaps ran away to join them; in any event, by the mid-1840s, Savage was a veteran mountain man, and one drawn to the then-burgeoning idea of Manifest Destiny that would culminate in the Mexican War, the occupation of California, and eventually the discovery of gold at Sutter's Mill in 1848.

Struck by the gold mania, Savage struck out for the southern Sierra, where he apparently hit paydirt on the Tuolumne River and points south. One account portrays Savage as a rather unusual Forty-Niner; where the more typical prospector was up to his knees and elbows in achingly cold streams of snow-melt with gold pan awash, Savage found a better way; apparently a gifted native linguist, with supposedly five wives from different central California tribes, Savage simply hired the natives to bring the gold to him.

"One pioneer," Solnit writes, "ran into him at this time 'under a brushwood tent . . . pouring gold dust into candle boxes by his side. Five hundred naked Indians . . . brought the dust to Savage, and in return for it received a bright piece of cloth or some beads.' Another explorer remembered that 'Jim Savage was the absolute and despotic ruler over thousands of Indians, extending all the way from Cosumnes [in the central Sierra foothills] to the Tejon Pass [across the Mojave Desert to the south] and was by them designated in their vernacular 'El Rey Guero'—the blond king. He called himself the Tulare King."

Solnit contends that Savage held his sway over the thousands of native Americans through parlor tricks and other sleights-of-hand suggesting supernatural powers, as well as his gift for languages. Nor did Savage neglect the proprieties of local politicking.

" 'It is related of him,' " Solnit quotes the famous California historian Hubert Howe Bancroft, " 'that he made it a point to marry a chief's daughter in every tribe; exchanged hardware and whiskey by weight, ounce for ounce, with the Indians for gold dust, and bet his weight in gold on the turn of a card in a San Francisco gambling house.' "

By 1850, Savage had relocated his trinkets-for-gold exchange post farther south on the Merced River, where he had relations with a band of Indians calling themselves the Miwok then living in the Merced River Canyon as it led up to Yosemite Valley.

But the aptly named Savage's depredations on the native population of central California couldn't last; early in 1850 a band of foothill Indians began stealing livestock to replenish the food supply that had been disrupted by their gold-digging new neighbors; one raid took place at Savage's Merced River trading post, and in December of the same year, another post was

wrecked; this time three employees were killed. Thus
began the Yosemite Indian War of 1851.

Having been the party attacked (although hardly the
more aggrieved), Savage immediately set out to round
up a militia to punish the offenders. Reports from his
many Indian sources told him that trouble was brewing
in the mountains among a band of Indians called the
Yosemite, which Savage thought meant "grizzly bear,"
implying that the tribe was named for its "lawless and
predatory character." But here Savage appeared to be
in error: not only were the Indians being hunted by the
hastily assembled militia—soon to be known as the
Mariposa Battalion—the wrong culprits, even Savage's
translation of their tribal name was wrong—very
wrong, as it turned out.

In any event, as the Mariposa Battalion under Savage and Lieutenant Treadwell Moore, 200 strong, clam-
bered up the Merced River canyon in pursuit of the
hostiles in early March of 1851, they were accompanied by a man named Lafayette Bunnell, who recorded
the valorous history of the battalion in a volume titled
*Discovery of the Yosemite and the Indian War of 1851
which Led to That Event*; it was Bunnell himself who
provided many of the Yosemite place names we know
today, such as Bridalveil Falls, and others.

The band of Miwok Indians "Major" Savage, Moore,
and Bunnell pursued was under the leadership of its
elder, Chief Ten-ie-ya, and were hardly grizzly bears,
to say nothing of being of "lawless and predatory character." Ordinarily, the Miwok weren't about to enter
the valley of the Yosemite, which was the domain

of still another band, the Ahwahneechee, named after the valley itself, the Ahwanhnee, meaning "big mouth." The Ahwahneechee were blood enemies of the Miwok: descendants of Paiutes who had spilled over the top of the Sierras into the big valley, the Ahwahneechees were known for their periodic raids on the more peaceful Miwok living in the canyons below.

But trapped between the vengeful Mariposa Battalion below and the Ahwahneechee above, Ten-ie-ya's Miwoks decided to head for the hills. Into the valley they went, across its wide floor, and then into the canyon that would come to be called Bloody Canyon, which we know today as Tenaya Canyon (the Park Services advises against climbing in Tenaya Canyon today as "dangerous and . . . strongly discouraged").

Near the summit, at a pristine alpine lake that would come to bear his name, Chief Ten-ie-ya halted. Bunnell recorded what happened next.

"When Ten-ie-ya reached the summit," Bunnell wrote, "he left his people and approached . . . the captain and a few of us. I called him up to us, and told him that we had given his name to the lake and river." Doubtless Bunnell thought he was honoring the chief, but Ten-ie-ya said it was hardly necessary; his people already knew what the lake and river were called, and it wasn't necessary for any white man to tell him what they were.

In return for such a place in posterity, Ten-ie-ya was informed that he and his people were to be brought back down to the central valley, there to live on a reservation for the rest of their lives.

Down the Miwok went, to settle on their meager reservation and eventually be wiped out by the gold diggers' diseases such as measles, syphilis, and diphtheria; this was how the West was won.

But Savage, while he might have won his war, missed the larger truth, according to Solnit, who draws upon the research of Craig Bates, a Yosemite Park ethnologist; for while it was true that the Miwok word for grizzly bear was "*uzumati*," the phonetically spelled Miwok word "*yosemite*" more naturally translates as "yohemiti"—the Miwok's characterization of their Ah-wahneechee enemies in the upper valley, and which meant: "some among them are killers."

NINE

YOSEMITE NATIONAL PARK: FEW,
probably none, of the horde of news media types who
descended on both El Portal and Modesto in the third
week of February of 1999 had any inkling of the dark
past that lay behind the name they used so frequently
to acquaint their audiences with what had happened, or
more exactly, what might have happened. Certainly it
was hardly the sort of name the National Park Service
wanted disseminated; already the service was beginning to field inquiries from reporters and the public
alike: was it safe to go to Yosemite?

On the day after the first Sund/Modesto/FBI press
conference, nearly a dozen Modesto detectives and two
dogs were out in force in the neighborhood where Carole's wallet had been found, interviewing residents
within a half-mile-square area of where the evidence
had been found. Nothing turned up, but the mere fact
that Carole's wallet had been found so far from where
Carole, Juli, and Silvina had last been seen almost cer-

tainly meant that some sort of foul play had occurred. After all, it wasn't very likely that Carole had simply lost her wallet and had just forgotten to let anyone know where she was.

That indeed was one of the main reasons why the FBI came into the case: there were only three realistic possibilities to account for the wallet's discovery in Modesto, and none of them were good. There was a distinct possibility of kidnapping; moreover, if a crime—such as carjacking or worse—had occurred inside Yosemite Park itself, the FBI would have jurisdiction.

The FBI office in this case was headquartered in Sacramento, California, the administrative center of the federal Eastern District of California, which encompassed a huge swatch of territory just east of the San Francisco Bay area from the Oregon border to Bakersfield. The FBI's Special Agent in Charge, James Maddock, headed a normal force of nearly 120 agents, augmented as required by specialists brought in from around the country.

Maddock, a 20-year veteran of the FBI, a lawyer, a triathlete, and a martial arts expert, was considered one of the FBI's brightest up-and-comers. In contrast to the traditional FBI public relations posture—there was a time, for example, back when Steven Stayner had first been kidnapped, that a local agent who found his name in the newspaper was likely to get an immediate assignment to someplace like East Butte, Montana—Maddock believed in the value of a public profile. Good relations with the press meant good relations with

the public; good relations with the public, Maddock
believed, meant more crimes solved. It was a long way
from the days of J. Edgar Hoover and Melvin Purvis,
that was for sure; Hoover had been so mad at Purvis's
good publicity after Purvis shot John Dillinger in the
1930s that he practically had Purvis drummed out of
the Bureau.

"Jim has a passion for his work and for protecting
the public safety," assistant FBI director John Collingwood told the *San Francisco Examiner* shortly after the
FBI entered the Sund/Pelosso case. "He also under-
stands the need for the Bureau to keep the public informed as much as it can legally. It's a delicate balance
when you have a profile case that's of tremendous concern to the public."

Maddock, 47, had already raised some eyebrows in
California when he first took over the Sacramento FBI
office in July of 1997. Shortly after moving in, he'd
announced publicly that his agents would be looking at
official corruption in the California State Legislature,
and quickly suited actions to words by dispatching
agents to interview lobbyists, apparently in alphabetical
order.

But Maddock was no stranger to controversy;
throughout much of 1995 and until his assignment to
Sacramento he'd served as the Bureau's point man in
a long-running controversy over the way the Bureau's
crime lab was being operated; a lab employee, Fred-
erick Whitehurst, had alleged that the lab's forensic sci-
entists were failing to follow accepted scientific
procedures in processing evidence, an allegation that

touched on such high-profile cases as the Oklahoma
City and World Trade Center bombings, among others.
It had been Maddock's job, as a member of the Bureau
general counsel's office, to oversee the Bureau's internal investigation of its lab's shortcomings, and also to
maintain contacts with the Justice Department's In-
spector General's office, and congressional committees
who were looking into the same matter.

"There was a lot of back and forth between the FBI
and the IG's office," Collingwood told the *Examiner.*
"There were factual disputes, there were interpretations
that we disagreed with. Jim was kind of in the middle
of that . . . it was a very tough situation."

It was so tough, in fact, that an influential Republi-
can senator, Charles Grassley of Iowa, claimed that
Maddock had tried to conceal information and witnesses from Congress in order to protect the FBI lab's
reputation. That wasn't the case at all, Maddock contended; he believed that one of the congressional investigators had tried to intimidate one of the lab
witnesses, and he was only trying to protect the person's rights.

Maddock was born in Massachusetts, and raised just
across the Potomac River from Washington, D.C., in
Alexandria, Virginia, and as such, he certainly was no
stranger to the way politics were played. After gradu-
ating from the University of Virginia in 1973, Maddock
had taken a job with the Internal Revenue Service as
an investigator, and after getting his law degree from
the university in 1979, began work for the FBI in 1980.
Over the years he had worked in Washington, New

York, Detroit, San Juan, Puerto Rico, and in Mississippi; for four years he'd supervised extremely sensistive undercover investigations conducted by the Bureau to make certain all the agency's regulations on covert operations were complied with, and in 1995 he'd been hired by the Bureau's general counsel office—the FBI's in-house legal staff—as one of four deputies, just in time to inherit the mess at the laboratory.

So, taken together, Maddock's varied background seemingly made him an ideal candidate to lead what was rapidly becoming one of the FBI's most publicized cases in recent years. By the time the next four months went by, the public became accustomed to seeing Maddock's face on the evening news, an event that would have been unheard of when J. Edgar Hoover was still in charge, back when little Steven Stayner was only an ordinary second-grader.

On the Monday following the FBI's entry into the case, the Sund/Carrington family held another press briefing; by now at least a dozen family members and friends had arrived in Modesto, setting up a headquarters, complete with a hotline for tips from the public, at the Modesto Holiday Inn.

Jens Sund took the opportunity to raise the prospect of the reward once again.

"You just hope somebody out there who has the information calls the number and gets the reward," he said, visibly haggard after six days and nights with no news. Asked why the reward was so large, Jens could only shrug.

"It's the price of a house," he said. "Who wouldn't exchange a house for their wife and daughter?"

In fact, the reward represented a sea change in the attitude toward the disappearances—from a possible accident to the strong suspicion of foul play.

"We are working it as a kidnapping or possible carjacking," said the FBI's spokesperson, Nick Rossi, from the Bureau's own headquarters several blocks away at the Modesto Doubletree Inn. "If it was just an adult, we would not be bringing so many resources to bear. But because minors were involved, it creates for us almost a presumption that a kidnapping may have occurred.

"We may still find that these women drove off the road," Rossi added, "but there are some indications of foul play. Certainly the location of the wallet, which was found in Modesto, shows the potential for foul play."

Potential—but that's just about all the FBI or anyone really had. The problem was: where to go when there were virtually no substantial leads? Without any confirmed sightings of the trio past Monday night, February 15, without any records as to their whereabouts, without the car, there was literally nothing to go on, and for all practical purposes, no place to start.

The Sund/Carrington forces had hired a private investigator, and with the Sund family's permission, the investigator set about trying to track activity in Carole's various bank and credit card accounts; that was one way to determine either her most recent whereabouts, or more important, whether anyone other than Carole had accessed the acounts anytime after Monday night. Sometimes, authorities knew, carjackers forced account holders to raid their own ATM accounts as part of the crime. But a review of Carole's last ATM transaction showed that it had taken place over the weekend in Merced, well before Jens had last talked to Carole on Monday night.

The car: the whole mystery came down to that. If only the car could be found, the authorities could begin to narrow their focus to at least make the best use of their resources. If the disappearance was the result of some criminal activity, locating the car could provide vital evidence as to the sort of person or persons investigators needed to focus on. Even the location of the car, if found, might be an important clue.

With that in mind, officials in Mariposa, assisted by the FBI and experts from the state's Office of Emergency Services, began a new search for the car—this one not predicated on the theory of an accident, but starting with the assumption that the car had been taken by the perpetrators, with or without the victims, and that it had been deliberately concealed by the criminals. That meant an entirely different kind of search, one in which the searchers had to pretend they were the bad guys, the better to look for a car no one wanted discovered.

TEN

THE SHIFT TO THE NOTION THAT Carole, Juli, and Silvina had been the victims of a crime necessitated two other considerations, as well.

The first was: what sort of person might the criminal be? Was he or she, for example, intimately familiar with the park and the El Portal area—in other words, a local? Or would the criminal be someone who had merely been passing through the park, and who had seized an opportunity to take advantage of someone who was vulnerable? If the latter were the case, how did the perpetrator get to the area? Did they leave their own vehicle and come back later? Or was there more than one person involved—someone who helped the kidnapper/carjacker/robber/whatever by picking them up once the deed was done?

Or finally, did the possible crime have anything to do with El Portal or the park at all? Had the whole thing taken place somewhere between Mariposa and Merced, or in Merced itself?

There were simply too many imponderables, and not enough facts.

But operating on the nearly always valid assumption that the best place to start anything was at the beginning, the FBI team under Maddock opened two separate investigative tracks during the last week of February: while a new and highly vigorous search was being conducted for the car, in or out of the park, and on the roads to and from it, for anyplace where a late-model vehicle might be hidden, a second focus was brought to bear on what so far seemed to be the epicenter of the event, whatever it was: Cedar Lodge at El Portal, which was the last place anyone had ever seen Carole, Juli, or Silvina alive. It was always best to start at the beginning and work outward, and for this reason Mariposa deputy sheriffs and FBI agents teamed up and began interviewing the Cedar Lodge staff, looking for anything that might generate a lead, and almost as important, evaluating those who had been nearest to the presumed victims when they were last seen.

There were three roads leading into and out of the park: Highway 41, which entered the park from the south, direct from Fresno; Highway 140, which came in from the west via Mariposa and El Portal; and Highway 120, which entered the park on the northwest and wound over the rim of the Sierras to Tioga Pass (Tenie-ya's objective before his capture by Jim Savage), which in turn emptied down the eastern escarpment of the mountains to Mono Lake, not far from the Nevada state line. But the eastern portion of Highway 120 that led to Tioga Pass was closed in winter because of snow buildup; and if Carole had indeed driven the car away from El Portal, it hardly seemed likely that she would take Highway 41 toward Fresno, when their appointment was in Stockton, so many miles in the other direction.

Although it appeared that Carole had planned to drive to Stockton on Tuesday, February 16, by way of Highway 140, information soon came from a park ranger that suggested that Carole and the girls might have decided to take Highway 120 instead.

The ranger, one of the myriad park workers and others questioned on Monday and Tuesday after the FBI came into the case, recalled talking with three women in a red car Tuesday morning, February 16; the trio had asked directions to Tuolumne Grove, a stand of large trees on the western edge of the park accessible only by Highway 120.

That highway climbs up the northern rim of Yosemite Valley, rising rapidly to more than a mile in elevation before reaching Crane Flat, a broad area overlooking the valley and an area called Big Meadow; the Tuolumne Grove was nearby—as were fueling facilities, which might have been an attraction to Carole, since the only other gas station within miles was in El Portal.

From Crane Flat and Tuolumne Grove it was less than five miles to the northwest entrance to the Park at Big Oak Flat. From there, Carole and the girls could have continued west on Highway 120 through Buck Meadows and Groveland, two hamlets on the way to

Modesto, before turning north on Highway 99 for the final run into Stockton.

The weather conditions, combined with the twists and turns of Highway 120, raised the possibility once more of a possible accident.

Further interviews seemed to indicate that others may have seen the car at Tuolumne Grove that Tuesday afternoon, and possibly at Buck Meadows later the same day.

"We have what we believe is credible information that they wanted to see the Tuolumne Grove of Big Trees," Maddock said, "and they asked directions on how to get to that part of the park." And the additional sighting at the grove that afternoon also appeared to be credible, Maddock added.

"What we are asking for is public assistance," Maddock said. "We would like anyone in Yosemite last Tuesday, especially anyone in the grove of Big Trees, to call the FBI."

Did that mean the FBI had returned to the theory of a simple accident? Or was the FBI still considering the case a possible kidnapping?

"There's a possibility they were kidnapped," Maddock said, "but there's been no ransom demand."

How long would the FBI stay with the case, in the absence of any substantial indication of what had happened?

"We're going to stay in this investigation," he said, "until we find the car or we find the victims or until we've exhausted every lead."

*   *   *

Even as the FBI and others stepped up their efforts along Highway 120, the Sund/Carrington family had moved into Modesto in full force. Using cellular phones, the dozen or so Sunds, Carringtons, and their friends combed the area of Modesto where Carole's wallet had been found, posting flyers about the reward and trying desperately to come up with some sort of lead. Jens's brother Ken Sund arrived and took charge. Soon the hotel had set aside a room for the hotline, and streams of volunteers from Modesto were coming in to answer the phones. The Polly Klass Foundation— formed by the family of the 13-year-old northern California girl who had been kidnapped and murdered several years earlier—stepped in with its own assistance, both with posting flyers and with helping the Sunds and Carringtons cope with the increasingly emotional situation.

The Wednesday he had first reported his wife, daughter, and Silvina missing, Jens told reporters, he'd had to make the "hardest call of my life." He'd telephoned Raquel Pelosso in Argentina to tell her that Silvina was lost.

Raquel had almost immediately taken a plane to California. By the Sunday after Carole's wallet had been found, Raquel had arrived in Modesto; that long-promised visit to see Carole in her own country had finally been made; only Carole wasn't there to greet her. Instead, the following day, Raquel met the media.

"Nothing like this has ever happened to us in Argentina," Raquel said. "We are not political people. If you know something about where she is, please tell us."

Two days later, Jose Pelosso, Raquel's husband and Silvina's father, also arrived in Modesto; soon the Pelossos were accompanied by representatives from the Argentinian Consulate in Los Angeles; Silvina's mysterious disappearance at the doorstep to one of the USA's most storied natural settings had become a national fixation in Argentina, leading the papers and the television broadcasts every day. The disappearance of three tourists in a land of enchantment had become international news.

ELEVEN

THE FIRST DAY'S SEARCH OF THE Highway 120 corridor went slowly; at first, authorities had only been able to draw on about 30 searchers, who were required to make their way carefully through dense underbrush in a yard-by-yard inspection off both sides of the highway. The searching was complicated by patches of snow and drifts that remained in the higher elevations.

"It's possible their car went off the road and is covered by snow now, so we're searching very carefully for that," said Larry Buffaloe, the head of the state's Office of Emergency Services.

Still, given the paucity of clues or even what route the women might have taken, there was the very real possibility that the searchers were wasting their time; the car could be anywhere, that was the real problem. But a big part of any investigation is elimination: if it could be shown that the car wasn't anywhere off the side of Highway 120, at least that possibility could be

eliminated, and efforts could be redirected. Another 60
searchers were drafted to continue the hunt for the following day.

As the search of Highway 120 continued, FBI and Mariposa County deputies began interviewing people in El
Portal, starting with the staff at Cedar Lodge.

Because of the season, the staff at the lodge was
relatively sparse, perhaps less than 20 people altogether. As the media frenzy advanced, the lodge staff
went through the four stages usually experienced by
ordinary people beset by a news media invasion: first,
fascination, followed by bemusement, then boredom at
the repetive questioning, and finally, sullen irritation at
all the intrusion.

Outside the lodge, the satellite trucks lined up, dishes
canted to the afternoon skies, along with the television
reporters with microphones in hand, each trying to update their audience on a story that didn't seem to be
going anywhere. All that anyone could say was that
three people had stayed at the Cedar Lodge on February
14 and 15, that they were last seen on the evening of
February 15, that people were searching for them, and
that the FBI had been called into the case, but that no
ransom demand had been received.

The repeated shots of Cedar Lodge in connection
with the disappearances began to irritate both the lodge
staff as well as the customers inside the restaurant and
lounge where the trio had last been seen. It was as if,
by association, the lodge was being portrayed as some

sort of sinister den of iniquity, where unwary tourists were at risk.

The omnipresence of the reporters, coupled with the law enforcement interviews, raised the level of tension around the lodge.

One by one, the employees of the lodge and restaurant were questioned. No, no one had seen Carole and the girls leave on Tuesday morning; no, they hadn't had breakfast at the restaurant; no one had yet cleaned the room where the trio stayed, at first because of the short staff, and not even later, because Mariposa deputies asked that the room be kept undisturbed until the authorities knew what they were dealing with. The only person who'd been in the room was the front desk employee who'd gone into the room on Tuesday afternoon to reclaim the VCR and the rental movie, and he hadn't noticed anything unusual. The beds appeared to have been made.

The agents and the Mariposa colleagues looked over the room once again. It was an ordinary motel room, just like millions of others across America, with one large carpeted room with two beds and a couch, and a small bathroom with a shower. Agents pulled the records of the telephone service for the room and found no surprises.

As the agents continued their interviews, an event would take place that would later loom large, although at the time no one gave it any special significance.

As it happened, one of the lodge employees was named Stayner—Cary Stayner, the older brother of little Steven, who had been kidnapped so many years before from the central valley town of Merced.

At 37 years old, Cary Stayner had grown into a strapping man—over six feet and close to 200 pounds. He'd always loved Yosemite, and in fact had been camping there on the day his little brother returned from his seven-year disappearance. At his age, Cary was one of the older members of the Cedar Lodge staff—generally regarded by his employers and his fellow workers as polite, reliable, among the more helpful and capable on the staff. He'd worked for the lodge since 1995, performing maintenance chores; indeed, there wasn't anything at the lodge Cary couldn't fix.

During their interviews with the lodge staff, the agents wanted to establish several things: first, whether any of the staff people had had encounters with Carole, Juli, or Silvina; and second, where each staff member was during the evening of February 15, when the trio had last been seen.

Because of the long-ago kidnapping of his brother, Cary's last name was familiar to the authorities. Indeed, Cary himself brought up the abduction of his brother so long ago.

"He volunteered information about it," said one officer familiar with the interview. "He said he felt for the people [the Sunds] because of what his own family had gone through."

But at the time that Carole, Juli, and Silvina were last seen, Cary himself hadn't been working at the lodge; in fact, he'd been one of those laid off temporarily because of the slack season.

Later, it would become unclear just how hard, if at

all, the agents initially pushed Cary in accounting for his whereabouts on the night of February 15. While it was clear he wasn't working at the lodge on the night in question, what wasn't clear—at least in reports published later—was whether the agents realized that Cary had permanent residence in a room over the restaurant during the time of the disappearance. Nor was it clear whether Cary's story about his own brother's abduction made much of an impression on his interviewers; often, such recollections of traumatic life events in an interview can provide a gateway for interviewers to load stress on an interview subject; sometimes, indeed, persistent emotional probing can lead to damning admissions or even confessions.

In any event, the team of agents and deputies interviewing Cary soon dismissed him from having any involvement in Carole, Juli, and Silvina's disappearance. In some ways, he was too old, too settled, too calm, they believed; in short, Cary Stayner, they believed, was just what he appeared to be: a competent maintenance man, a laid-back hippie-type, someone without grand ambitions who simply enjoyed living near Yosemite for the hiking and swimming opportunities that seemed to be at the center of his existence.

That assessment, as matters were to turn out, was as wildly wrong as it could be.

By Saturday, February 27—12 days after Carole, Juli, and Silvina were last seen—James Maddock and his fellow law enforcement authorities decided for the time being to scale back the search for the car. So far, the efforts of 70 searchers had turned up nine different abandoned or stolen vehicles, none of which was the right one.

If the car couldn't be found, the next step was to try to find witnesses who might have seen the trio after the night of February 15. To that end, teams of agents and detectives stopped at dozens of restaurants, filling stations, and motels up and down the major routes in the area: Highway 120 where it headed toward Highway 99, on Highway 99 itself, Highway 132 (which ran directly into Modesto from midway between Highway 140 and Highway 120), and Highway 108, which crossed the Sierra north of the park by way of Sonora Pass. These contacts resulted in a slew of possible sightings, but none of them stood out as particularly credible; by now, the publicity over the trio's disappearance, coupled with the news about the reward, had a number of people seeing things.

The lack of any substantial information had reinforced in Maddock's mind the idea that almost certainly a crime had been committed. The absence of the car, the discovery of the wallet, and most important, the fact that Carole had been gone for almost two weeks without being heard from all stood as circumstantial evidence that the women had met with some form of foul play, probaly fatal.

"We are all operating under the assumption that a crime did occur," he said.

At a press conference on Saturday, February 27, Maddock said his agency would now put the possibility of a crime at the forefront of their efforts; to that end, he announced that a pair of psychological profilers from the Bureau would be arriving to help assess the situation. So far, Maddock added, his agents had interviewed a number of people, and had eliminated several as potential suspects in the disappearance.

By the middle of the week, Maddock was able to provide some idea of the effort that had been undertaken so far. At least 60 agents had been assigned to the case to assist police in Modesto and Stockton. As of the first of the week, more than 900 tips had been received, which together generated 223 leads to be checked out. Altogther, searchers had combed more than 7,000 square miles, on foot, by snowshoe, snowmobile, and from the air.

In the absence of any hard evidence other than Carole's black leather wallet, Maddock said, his agency would have to do the reverse of most investigations: first, form a theory of what might have happened, and then work the theory forward and backward to see whether any suspects might fit the bill.

Maddock said the FBI had developed two different theories to start with: one, a crime of opportunity, such as a carjacking or robbery gone bad, in which the events occurred at random as a result of an impulse; and second, that the crime was planned in advance, such as a kidnapping, or possibly a long-term stalking.

To check these theories, Maddock said, agents had retraced the Sund/Pelosso route in Stockton on the Saturday before the disappearance; had examined video tape from ATM and mini-mart security cameras to see whether any record of Carole, Juli, or Silvina might be found; had questioned scores of residents and business owners near where Carole's wallet had been found; had intensively interviewed nearly two dozen people, including Jens; had given a number of polygraph tests; and had conducted a thorough search of Carole and Jens' home and offices in Eureka on the chance that some scrap of paper or note there might shed light on what had happened.

An accident, Maddock added, had virtually been ruled out.

"If it was an accident," he said, "the accident would've occurred in an area that was searched."

What Maddock did not tell reporters at the time was that one possible lead had turned up that might have to do with Carole's wallet. Twice in the week following Carole's disappearance, it turned out, someone had called Wells Fargo Bank, inquiring about Carole Sund's account status; having first faced an automated menu, the caller was soon transferred to a human being at the bank, who realized that she was talking to a woman. But the caller, whoever she was, was unable to satisfy the bank's security procedures, and the call was terminated.

Who made these calls? The bank's computer system had logged almost 800,000 calls during the week in question; and while one part of the computer registered the incoming caller's number, it wasn't technically possible to match the incoming number to the specific inquiries on Carole's account. To get there, someone would have to check the incoming calls by hand for the approximate times of the calls, to see where the calls had come from. That would be a laborious process, and one that was still ongoing as the fall of 1999 arrived. Still, the investigators believed the calls showed there had to be at least two people involved in the disappearances: at least one to control the victims, and a second, female accomplice to make the calls to the bank. As of September of 1999, the calls still remained a mystery.

Meanwhile, Jens Sund and his family had taken over a conference room at the Holiday Inn in Modesto, using it as a headquarters to process the tips that kept coming into their hotline, and to keep the news media abreast of any developments in the case. Jens knew, as did his father-in-law Francis Carrington, that keeping the story alive in the media was one way to make sure that if anyone knew anything, they might come forward. The conference room was decorated with photos of the Sund and Pelosso families, going back to the trip to Argentina made by the Sunds in 1985.

By now, Jens had been interviewed countless times, including appearances on *America's Most Wanted*, *Hard Copy*, *Inside Edition* and *Good Morning America*. Apart from the strain of being in the public eye, however much he sought it, the emptiness of his situation was beginning to take a hard toll on Jens. In the most visceral way possible, the silence was killing Jens Sund, just as it had Del and Kay Stayner so many years before. It was the not knowing that was the poison, the paralysis that constantly threatened to dim the will; if only he could do something, but there was nothing to do but wait.

"I could," he told reporter Eric Brazil of the *San Francisco Examiner*, "have a hundred people here right now to search, but we don't know where to search."

Although he didn't say so directly, it was also clear that Jens was losing hope. When he returned to Eureka to take his three remaining children back to school, he said, it struck him: "Everything's changed, my whole life." While in Eureka, he went through Carole's office, and noticed, as if for the first time, how organized everything was. This was such a part of his life: Carole the organizer, everything arranged just so. And now this force for order, for normalcy, was gone, disappeared, vanished. He realized, he continued, that the outlook wasn't good for his wife's survival, and he told the other children that.

"I told them it may be bad," he said. "It may be the worst news we've ever had. It's been so many days . . . that we may get the worst news. I believe they understand."

Jens had just about given up on speculating; it was a form of imagination that did no good.

"I have no theories," he told Brazil. "I've heard so many different theories that I just don't know. I'd rather wait and see what happens."

The next day, in the small hours of the morning, Jens decided to try to put his feelings into the written word for the *Examiner*.

"How do I feel? I have been asked this question countless times during the past two weeks by the many reporters who have taken a personal interest in helping me find my family."

It was, he said, like a nightmare one couldn't awaken from.

"And so at 3:00 A.M. I find myself reflecting on how I feel, awakened again to my nightmare, and again wondering where they are."

Jens went on to describe his wife.

"Carole is a doer. From the first time we met in high school at the age of seventeen, I realized this. Carole would rather change something or at least try and make a difference rather than sit back and complain."

Carole, Jens continued, was dedicated to making things better for children; she'd volunteered for a county review board that oversaw the handling of abused and neglected children; later she'd volunteered for the court-appointed guardian program for children's welfare in the Humboldt County court system. She'd served on a board overseeing a county program for adoptions.

Carole was the leader in the Sund family, Jens continued; he still "impulsively" tried to telephone her whenever he had a problem to be ironed out. With Carole gone, Jens said he now realized, "I am heading into uncharted territory.

"How do I feel as I sit here helplessly in Modesto, speaking out publicly in the hope that these efforts may somehow reach someone, anyone who may offer a tip, a lead, or possibly my wish, to extricate themselves from something they never wanted to be a part of?

"Three children need me, seven hours away, yet here I wait in Modesto answering the question . . . how do you feel?"

The answer, Jens thus suggested, should have been obvious.

TWELVE

A WEEK PASSED SINCE JENS SUND had bared his soul in the *Examiner*, and still nothing seemed to be happening. The car was still missing, and the $250,000 reward remained unclaimed. But as the second week of March arrived, a flurry of rumors swept through the 680-odd permanent residents of El Portal: something big was about to happen.

In fact, the FBI had hardly been idle during the previous two weeks. Having adopted an inductive method to their investigation—creating a theory and looking for facts to support it—the FBI and the local authorities had dipped into the obvious wellspring of possible facts: the criminal histories of those closest to the most likely scene of the crime, El Portal itself.

Indeed, the FBI with the cooperation of the Mariposa authorities, had decided on a thorough sweep of all parolees and probationers in the county. If the evidence couldn't lead them to the crime scene, perhaps the known criminals could.

Of the 16,000 or so permanent residents of Mariposa County, there were a number of individuals on parole; a state-compiled list of registered sex offenders totaled 55 individuals in the county—including, as it turned out, a prominent member of the Mariposa Chamber of Commerce. Who knew what might turn up if enough rocks were turned over?

If, as one theory held, the crime was one of opportunity, rather than advance planning, the task was to review those with previous criminal histories to see who might be capable of kidnapping and possibly murdering three people; at the very least, those with a predilection for breaking the law might be made to account for their whereabouts during the critical days.

One condition of parole and probation in California grants law enforcement the right to conduct searches without warrant; indeed, a probationer or parolee must account for his or her whereabouts whenever requested to do so by a law enforcement official. The Great Mariposa County Parole Sweep of 1999 was about to net some interesting subjects, indeed. Ideally, some subjects might be isolated who had the capability of committing crimes associated with the trio's disappearance, who had no verifiable alibi, and—was it too much to hope for?—also some record of associations in the Modesto area. Once those individuals were identified, the game of sweatbox could commence.

One of the first to fall into the net was a worker at the restaurant at Cedar Lodge, one Billy Joe Strange. Billy Joe, 38, was the night cleanup man at the restaurant where Juli and Silvina had been eating hamburgers the night they were last seen. A former worker at the local El Portal garage, Strange had been quietly picked. up the previous Friday night for violating his parole by reportedly being drunk in the restaurant's lounge. Billy Joe was on parole for an earlier domestic violence conviction.

Billy Joe's arrest had many in El Portal angry; after all, he was pretty much a regular at the lounge, and if drinking was a violable offense, he should have been nabbed months, if not years earlier. To many, it seemed that the authorities were just looking for an excuse to grab someone, anyone. But the Sweep was in full-press mode, and Billy Joe's transgression gave the authorities the opportunity to yank him in and subject his small cabin and his car to a thorough search. As it happened, Billy Joe's girlfriend was the night clerk at the Cedar Lodge; her car was seized for examination as well.

Within hours of his arrest, the searching officers had also seized a small amount of marijuana from Strange's cabin—another no-no for a parolee—and had taken substantial swatches of carpet from the interior of the small house.

Not only was Strange stashed in the Mariposa County jail, a number of his friends were given polygraph tests over the weekend, a move that outraged many of Billy Joe's friends in El Portal.

"They are really fishing," one of Billy Joe's pals told the *San Francisco Chronicle*. "I don't see how they can make anything stick. There's nothing there." And Strange's girlfriend, the night clerk at the motel, was particularly upset at the way the agents and parole officers had swept through their tiny dwelling.

"All I know," she said, "is that me and Billy didn't have nothing to do with the disappearance of that family." One friend of Billy Joe's told the *Examiner* that Billy Joe had prevously been interviewed several times in connection with the disappearance, and claimed that Strange had told him that he'd failed a lie detector test. But lying about drinking or smoking marijuana was one thing; lying about kidnapping and murder was another matter entirely.

Billy Joe's friend told the *Examiner* that Strange hadn't helped himself very much earlier in the week; when agents came into the motel lounge looking for him, he jumped off his stool and ran away.

"He was tired of being hassled," Billy Joe's friend explained, "and they wanted to question him again and he just ran." A few days later they grabbed him for drinking in violation of his probation, which led to the discovery of the marijuana and his subsequent arrest.

Billy Joe's arrest was one factor in the rumors that were sweeping through El Portal by mid-March; another was a statement from Jens Sund himself. In Modesto, Jens confided to reporters that he'd been given devastating news by the FBI.

"My worst possible fears have come true," Jens said. "They've made some discoveries, but I'm not supposed to comment on it. It doesn't look good for my family."

Thus, Jens's remarks, coupled with Billy Joe Strange's arrest and the search of his house and car, fueled the speculation that a break in the case had either occurred or was imminent. That was just what the newspeople had been waiting for so long; all those days in front of the Cedar Lodge with nothing to say were wearing thin on reporters and news producers alike.

But the day after his remarks, Jens recanted, saying that no matter what else had so far happened, the authorities still had yet to find any real evidence of any crime besides the recovery of Carole's wallet.

"I've been on an emotional roller coaster," Jens said. "You caught me in one of my lows. It drains me. You get the feeling that maybe there was some kind of answer. You get strung out, expectant, and hopeful, and you just kind of let loose."

Although it wasn't made clear, it seemed obvious that the violation of Billy Joe's parole, his arrest, and the thorough search of his house and car had been communicated to Jens, and that Jens's expectations had risen dramatically, only to be dashed when a confession (or even solid evidence) wasn't forthcoming from Bill Joe Strange.

The FBI moved quickly to pour cold water on the rumors, in part because of the prospect that still more parolees would soon be pulled in for grilling. If every time a potential bad guy was hauled in for questioning a news media firestorm erupted, nothing would get accomplished, the FBI knew.

"There are no major new developments to report," the FBI's Nick Rossi said. "Rumors that the FBI has discovered the bodies of the victims or their vehicle are false."

The rumors about the possible discovery of the bodies undoubtedly stemmed from the fact that teams of

FBI agents had begun combing the wooded hillsides near Cedar Lodge itself; the obvious implication was that the remains of Carole, Juli, and Silvina might be found nearby in shallow graves. These rumors were pumped up by unconfirmed talk that agents were digging in certain areas near the lodge.

"The investigative process that we've been pursuing is one of identifying and then eliminating possibilities," Rossi said. "It's only natural that we would focus on the area where they were last seen."

But at least with Billy Joe in the slammer, the reporters had something new to focus on. Soon reporters were working down Billy Joe's backtrail to see what had made him of such interest to the authorities. Court records in Mariposa led to Bill Joe's former mother-in-law, who clearly had no great affection for her former son-in-law.

"I'm not surprised his name has come up," she told the *Examiner*. "I've suspected it would from the get-go." It turned out that Billy Joe had twice been convicted of domestic violence, beating both his ex-wife and her sister. Sentenced to prison in April of 1996, Billy Joe had been released in July of 1997. While on parole from the first conviction, Billy Joe went after his wife once more in December of the same year, and went back to prison until April of 1998.

The root of Strange's problem, however, appeared to be alcohol. His former mother-in-law described him as a person with a mean temper that wasn't improved by liquor.

The mother-in-law's assessment of Billy Joe notwithstanding, many in El Portal told reporters they considered Billy Joe a good guy, quiet and friendly—hardly the sort of demeanor one might expect of a potential triple kidnapper/murderer, let alone someone capable of executing what was looking more and more like the perfect crime. In fact, in El Portal there were vastly more votes for Billy's innocence than guilt.

The owner of a nearby trailer park, where Billy Joe lived, was livid over the presence of the FBI on his property during the search.

"The FBI and the searchers, about twenty-four of them," the owner told the *Chronicle*, "just showed up Tuesday morning and started walking shoulder to shoulder through my RV park. It was really irritating. They didn't say a thing. They just started walking."

It wasn't only the FBI who took criticism for the bust of Billy Joe; so, too, did the news media, for publicizing his name and suggesting that he'd had something to do with the Sund/Pelosso disappearances. Soon reporters in El Portal were being reminded of the saga of Richard Jewell, the Atlanta security guard who was incorrectly labeled a suspect by the FBI and the media in the Atlanta Olympic bombing; the same situation applied to Billy Joe, his friends said.

But that didn't mean that Billy Joe wasn't somehow peripherally involved in the disappearance, perhaps without even knowing how. That was one reason the FBI had searched his house and his vehicles: in case Billy Joe had somehow come into possession of something belonging to one of the victims.

"We're forced to treat a large number of things as

potential evidence," the FBI's Rossi explained, "which in the end may not pan out. We're going through the process of elimination."

The day after the rumors blew up and were then extinguished, the FBI's James Maddock held another press conference.

"We felt almost certain," Maddock said, "that the women were the victims of a violent crime. After this length of time, it would be a miracle if the victims were recovered alive."

Meanwhile, Maddock said, the search was still going on, although on a lesser scale. By this point, he said, the searchers were looking for bodies—in old mine shafts and tunnels, and in potential shallow graves. The problem, Maddock pointed out, was the entire countryside was a vast repository of potential hiding places.

But Maddock said he was increasingly convinced of one thing: whatever had happened to Carole, Juli, and Silvina, it had happened at or around Cedar Lodge.

"I can tell you," Maddock said, "that we feel almost certain that the women were the victims of a violent crime. We are now focusing on one theory that we believe to be the most likely scenario.

"That scenario includes a violent crime occuring at or near the Cedar Lodge on the evening of Monday, February 15 or during the early morning hours of Tuesday, February 16."

THIRTEEN

THEORIES, POSSIBILITIES, ELIMINA-
tions: that's what it still all came down to, Maddock
was the first to admit.

"We have not arrested anyone," he said. "No one
has been charged in connection with the missing persons. We have not recovered the missing people. We
have not found the car."

The car, the damned car. If only it would turn up,
the authorities could pull away from their theories, possibilities, and eliminations and get down to some
heavy-duty investigating. It seemed completely
impossible that the entire vehicle could have disappeared without a trace. While some thought the car
might have been stripped and parted out, surely by now
some piece of it would have surfaced. That left only
the possibility that the car had been dismantled and the
parts strewn to the four corners of the earth in order to
conceal it, and while searchers had been instructed to
keep an eye out for buried car parts, that scenario

seemed entirely too elaborate, far too planned, with far too many people involved. Conspiracy theories were one thing, but they were all too easy to take much too far.

As Maddock suggested, the FBI had just about given up the idea that the disappearance was a planned event; there was seemingly too little margin for error in some sort of plot. There was first of all the question of how the perpetrator or perpetrators were able to control all three victims at the same time in such a narrow window of opportunity. Everything pointed to a random event, a spur-of-the-moment crime occasioned by impulse and pure chance.

That wasn't how people in El Portal saw matters, however, where a groundswell of support for Billy Joe Strange continued to build.

"Ain't nobody from up here involved with it, I can tell you that," Paul Miller, the local gas station manager and a long-time friend of Billy Joe's told the *Examiner*. "This would have been done by a pro. It's not someone from here."

And a waitress at the restaurant complained that Billy Joe's arrest was giving the entire community a black eye. "Billy Joe's a part of this community, and he hasn't been charged with anything," she said. "Yet everytime they show a picture of the missing . . . on TV, they show Billy Joe's picture right next to it. It's not fair."

Miller agreed.

"He's not a suspect. The only thing they have to go on is he's on parole. He's a good old boy, and he's done a lot to help people in the community here."

All of the attention from the FBI and the news media on El Portal, many agreed, was becoming intolerable, and while nearly everyone hoped the missing women would be found, they also hoped the federals and their media circus would get out of town.

They were soon to get their wish.

It still kept coming back to the car: if only someone could find it, then some answers might be found, and progress could begin to be made. To that end, Carole's father, Francis Carrington, offered an additional $50,000 reward for anyone who could locate the vehicle.

Carrington's reasoning was quite sound; by this point, the FBI was convinced that more than one person had to be involved in the disappearances. It beggared all reason to believe that one person, acting alone, could somehow get control of three active, healthy women. Carole Sund was a good-sized woman, at nearly 160 pounds, and certainly no shrinking violet. Juli herself weighed nearly 140 pounds. It stood to reason that one person acting alone in trying to get control of the three had a good chance of getting his clock cleaned. At the very least, it was likely one or more would make a break for freedom. The most reasonable scenario had at least two abductors, if not more. And finally, there was the still-perplexing issue of transportation: if the kidnappers had taken the Sund rental car, whatever became of their own transportation?

If more than one person was involved, which seemed

most likely, the chances were great that someone would tell someone else; sooner or later, the story, or at least enough of it to make sense, would filter out to someone who wasn't involved. A $50,000 reward for the finding of the car was a powerful inducement.

But for the Sunds and Carringtons, money was only one weapon in the arsenal used to keep the unknown fate of the missing women before the public. Plans were made to assemble a large rally in downtown Modesto for the following Sunday. Drawing on the support of the Polly Klaas Foundation and a similar group named after another child missing from the early 1980s, Amber Schwartz, the idea was to keep the public's focus on the missing Carole, Juli, and Silvina. Even as it was, calls were still coming into the Sund/Carrington hotline at the Holiday Inn at a rate of about 25 a day. All of these tips had to be screened, then passed onto the FBI, which had their own staff of screeners getting similar calls.

"I guess it's a way to feel accomplishment," said Francis Carrington of the rally, "that you've got to do something that might help." But Francis was beginning to have his doubts about the efficacy of the investigation so far. In a brief moment of discouragement, Francis said he didn't believe that the FBI knew anything for sure.

"I don't think they know anything," Francis told the *Examiner*. "We've been chasing false leads." That was one reason for the reward for information leading to the car; at least, if the car was found, officials would have something solid to work with.

On Sunday, March 14, after a march from the FBI's headquarters at the Doubletree Inn, nearly 1,000 people turned out at Gracedada Park in downtown Modesto to conduct a vigil for Carole, Juli, and Silvina's safe return. Scores of volunteers painted signs reading "VIGIL FOR HOPE," while others circulated still more of flyers, this one announcing the $50,000 reward for locating the car. FBI agents attended the rally as well; who knew—maybe the kidnapper/carjacker or whatever he was might also attend?

Jens Sund did not attend the rally. Emotionally exhausted, still recovering from his outburst of several days earlier, Jens went back to Eureka to be with his remaining children; after nearly a month in Modesto, with his hopes alternately rising and ebbing, Jens simply had to decompress. From that point forward, his brother Ken and in-laws Francis and Carole Carrington would take the point in keeping the disappearances in the public eye.

One of those who spoke at the rally was Joe Klass, the grandfather of the kidnapped and murdered Polly Klass, whose case had horrified the nation after she was taken from a teenage girls' slumber party in Petaluma earlier in the '90s. Still others who had lost loved ones to unexplained fates were also present: Kim Swartz, whose seven-year-old daughter was kidnapped in 1988 from a Bay Area suburb, and Minnie Norrell, whose 14-year-old daughter was murdered in 1998 in Pittsburg, California. Each of the missing or dead had commanded momentary public attention for a time, something that happened to some distant stranger; it was only when their names were assembled together that one realized truly what an epidemic of violence against children we have in America. It was a crowd whose feelings Del and Kay Stayner, at home in Atwater, California, near Merced, would have understood all too well.

"This poor family . . . surrounded by members of other families in a bond of love that exists between those who have had loved ones stolen," Joe Klass said. "A common bond of agony . . . a common bond of love.

"In the name of Carol, Juli, and Silvina, let us dedicate ourselves to a new crusade for peace in the most violent nation on earth. Why is this the country where it's unsafe for a twelve-year-old to walk her dog? Why is this the country where it's unsafe for a fifteen-year-old and a mother and a daughter to visit Yosemite National Park?"

Joe Klass concluded with a warning.

"Don't ever think you're safe, until we learn as a nation to solve this problem."

MISSING

JULIE SUND   CAROLE SUND   SILVINA PELOSSO

1999 PONTIAC GRAND PRIX
CALIFORNIA LICENSE 4BMV025

ANYONE WITH INFORMATION SHOULD CALL
THE FEDERAL BUREAU OF INVESTIGATION
AT 1 800 435-7883
TOLL FREE

A poster released by the FBI after agents joined the search for Carole Sund, Juli Sund, and Silvina Pelosso in February 1999.
(AP/Wide World Photos)

Sixteen-year-old Argentine exchange student Silvina Pelosso poses amidst Yosemite's grandeur with Juli Sund, (left) and with Carole Sund (below) days before all three were murdered.
(AP/Wide World Photos)

The Cedar Lodge in El Portal, CA.
(AP/Wide World Photos)

The booth where Carole and Juli Sund sat with Silvina
Pelosso on the night they were last seen.
(AP/Wide World Photos)

Jens Sund, Carole's husband and Juli's father, speaks at a news conference in Modesto, CA, almost a month after the women disappeared on February 15th. (AP/Wide World Photos)

Next of kin. Left to right: Jose and Raquel Pelosso, Silvina's parents; Francis and Carole Carrington, Carole Sund's parents/ Juli Sund's grandparents. (AP/Wide World Photos)

A flatbed truck carries the remains of Carole Sund's rental car down Highway 108, near Sierra Village. On March 20th, authorities found the badly burned vehicle and, in its trunk, the bodies of Silvina Pelosso and Carole Sund. (AP/Wide World Photos)

Lake Don Pedro. Juli Sund's body was found nearby on March 25th, 1999.
(AP/Wide World Photos)

A simple memorial left near the site where searchers found Juli Sund's remains.
(AP/Wide World Photos)

Stockton, California: pallbearers lift the body of Silvina Pelosso onto a plane for the first leg of her grim return voyage to Argentina.
(AP/Wide World Photos)

Joie Ruth Armstrong, the Yosemite Institute naturalist who was found beheaded in July 1999. (AP/Wide World Photos)

Two of Joie Armstrong's colleagues at the Yosemite Institute embrace after hearing news of her murder. (AP/Wide World Photos)

Park Ranger Ryan Levins stands at a roadblock in Yosemite after Joie Armstrong's body was found. (AP/Wide World Photos)

FBI Special Agent James Maddock addresses a news conference in Yosemite National Park after Armstrong's murder. Chief Ranger Bob Andrews stands to his right. Behind them is the famous Half Dome. (AP/Wide World Photos)

Confessed serial killer
Cary Anthony Stayner.
(AP/Wide World Photos)

Steven Stayner in 1981. Steven,
the brother of Cary Stayner who
was abducted by a pederast in
1972, made national headlines
and became the subject of the
TV movie "I Know My Name Is
Steven," after escaping his cap-
tor and notifying authorities.
(AP/Wide World Photos)

The trailer home
in Atwater, CA,
where Cary
Stayner lived
before moving to
El Portal.
(AP/Wide World
Photos)

August 1999: Fresno police escort the van carrying Cary Stayner
to the Federal Building.
(AP/Wide World Photos)

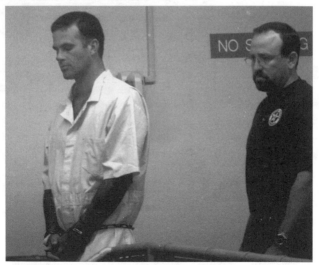

Cary Stayner in the Fresno County jail.
(AP/Wide World Photos)

FOURTEEN

IT SOON LEAKED OUT THAT BILLY Joe Strange wasn't the only El Portal parolee the authorities had their eye on as the investigation continued.

A few days after picking up Billy Joe, the FBI zeroed in on one of Billy Joe's friends, Darrell Stephens, 55, who sometimes shared the small El Portal cabin with Billy Joe and his girlfriend, the desk clerk.

Checking Stephens's background showed that he'd been convicted of rape and robbery in southern California nearly 20 years earlier, but that he was one of those who failed to register as a sex offender. It also appeared that he had committed other crimes years before in Texas. The FBI put the word out to the Mariposa deputies, along with a suggestion that Stephens might be worth talking to, and by Sunday, March 15, even as the crowd was holding its vigil in Modesto, Stephens was under lock and key in the Mariposa county jail, along with his old pal, Billy Joe Strange.

In the days before his own arrest, Stephens had been

one of those who had defended Billy Joe.

"The FBI has been hassling me and everyone Billy and I know," Stephens told the *San Francisco Chronicle*, "asking us all kinds of questions, but none of us knows anything about what happened to those women." And in an interview with the Fresno *Bee*, Stephens elaborated.

"They asked me, do I know where the bodies are? Did I have any knowledge of their disappearance? Over and over and over," he said. Agents had seized a knife from the cabin he and Billy Joe sometimes shared, along with carpet swatches. Both he and Billy Joe had taken lie detector tests, and he'd passed, Stephens claimed. Stephens continued to insist that neither he nor Billy Joe had anything to do with the disappearances.

The vigil in Modesto provided the news reporters with their first extended opportunity to size up the Pelossos, Jose and Raquel. The Pelossos were a fairly well-off family in Argentina, with interests in a bottling plant and cattle ranches; they had an older daughter, Paula, who had spent some time in the United States before Silvina's visit.

The worst of their plight, Raquel told the *Examiner*'s Erin McCormick, was the waiting; but both Pelossos were grateful for the kindness of the people of Modesto.

"This has shown me the worst part of America and the best part of America," Raquel said. "If someone attacked my daughter and her friend Juli and perhaps killed them, there must be some bad people here. On the other hand, so many people have been wonderful to us."

By this time, having appeared on television numerous times, the Pelossos were recognizable to many people in Modesto. Often, when they went out to dinner, fellow diners picked up their check.

"The FBI said only a miracle can bring them back. Okay, then: I believe in miracles."

The worst thing that could happen, she added, would be for the Pelossos to have to return to Argentina without ever knowing what had happened to their daughter.

The disappearance of Silvina along with the others continued to be big news back in Argentina. A team of reporters from that country had descended on Modesto, along with a deputy Argentine consul, Raul Guastavino from Los Angeles; Guastavino was helping the Pelossos cope with the media influx, and with the U.S. law enforcement agencies.

"People [in Argentina] are very upset," Guastavino told McCormick. "This is a middle-class family, who sent a teenaged daughter to the United States, a place we in Argentina perceive as being very safe. Now she's disappeared under mysterious circumstances." As a result, he said, the Argentina news media were covering the events comprehensively.

Perhaps showing just a bit of unfamiliarity with the vastness of the terrain encompassed by the park and its surroundings, state authorities in Argentina dispatched three Argentinian police officers trained in mountain rescues to help search for the trio. The FBI and its local counterparts were both perplexed and bemused by the officers' arrival; by that point it was quite clear that whatever had happened to Carole, Juli and Silvina, they weren't stranded on some mountain ledge somewhere in Yosemite Park.

"Because of the exposure this case is getting in Argentina, local authorities felt they had to do something," Guastavino told McCormick.

The FBI's Nick Rossi indicated that ways were being sought to integrate the three Argentinian officers into their efforts, but that it wasn't easy bringing the three up to speed after all that had happened.

Still, the vigil was heartening to the Sunds and Carringtons, as well as the Pelossos; it showed that people cared.

Now began a critical week in the course of the investigation, although few knew it at the time. A series of events ensued, some important, some not; the decisions taken in response to each were to have profound impacts on subsequent events.

For one, an anonymous letter was put into the mail; written in block letters on a loose-leafed notepage, the missive taunted the FBI for its failure to accomplish anything so far, and provided detailed information on the location of Juli Sund's body. For some reason, however, the letter was misdirected, either by a faulty address by the writer, a miscue by the Post Office, or some other human error. As a result, the letter was not to surface for ten more days; by that time, a lot of other things had happened.

LONG BARN

FIFTEEN

JUST A BIT AFTER 1:00 P.M. ON THE Tuesday following the vigil in Modesto, 40-year-old Michael Larwick, a man with a long history of behaving badly, was driving a yellow Camaro not far from the place where Carole Sund's wallet had been found almost a month before. Larwick glanced up at his rearview mirror and saw that he'd just been made by a cruising Modesto police officer.

Officer Steve Silva had noticed that the license tag on the yellow Camaro was expired. Silva flipped on his red lights, intending to check the driver out and probably give him a ticket; he didn't have the slightest idea of what he was in for.

As soon as Silva hit his red lights, Larwick jammed the gas pedal to the floor and began careening through the residential streets of northwest Modesto, with Silva in pursuit. Reaching speeds up to 80 miles an hour, the Camaro took a curve on two wheels, crashed into a parked van, and spun to a stop in the parking lot of a nearby convenience store. Silva fishtailed his patrol car to a stop and wasn't far behind.

Larwick jumped out of the Camaro and started running away, but not before firing between five and ten shots at Silva. Silva first reported to the police dispatcher that he was in foot pursuit, then that shots were being fired, and then, about 16 seconds later, that he was hit.

Probably nothing accelerates the adrenaline of a police patrol officer as the news that a fellow officer has been fired upon, and hit. Within seconds of the shooting, Modesto patrol cars began arriving at the scene. It soon became clear that the shooter had run down a residential street, Bridle Path Lane, and had broken into a house there.

Rushing into an unfamiliar house occupied by a man with a gun who had already shot one police officer wasn't the smartest move at that point, and the Modesto Police were well aware of that. Such things required time and planning: first, surrounding the house to make sure the shooter didn't get away, and secondly, getting all the civilians nearby to a safe location in case the lead started flying.

At just that moment, Brandi Grijalva, whose parents owned the house—they'd moved in just two months earlier—drove up the street, preparing to go inside. The police stopped her, and told her that a suspected cop-shooter was barricaded inside.

Brandi, naturally excited, called her mother at a Modesto insurance agency. Because of the excitement, Brandi's message was a bit garbled; Jeanne Grijalva, her mother, formed the impression that Brandi herself was inside the house with the gunman. Jeanne in turn called her husband, John Grijalva, at his job in Campbell, California, nearly 100 miles away. John wasn't available, so Jeanne left a message: "John," Jeanne said, "I need you. There's been a shooting and the guy is still in our house." Grijalva's first impression was that his daughter was the hostage of some madman.

Jeanne by this time had again talked with Brandi, and had realized that Brandi wasn't in the house after all; when John called Jeanne back, he realized that it was the *house* that was at risk, not his family. Nevertheless, John got in his car and made the nearly two-hour drive home to see what was going on. All the way there he kept thinking how close a call it had been: if Brandi had arrived only a few minutes sooner, she would have been trapped in the house with the crazed gunman, with the Modesto SWAT team arranged outside ready to riddle the house with high-powered bullets.

Meanwhile, the Modesto police and Larwick settled in for a siege. Larwick scouted the house, found a rear closet to hole up in, made himself a sandwich from the Grijalva's refrigerator, helped himself to a bag of barbecue potato chips, and opened a bottle of champagne.

All afternoon, both sides waited for something to happen, with the police making periodic demands for the shooter to come out with his hands up. But Larwick refused to budge.

Finally, a bit after two in the morning, the police began firing tear gas rounds into the house—at least

30, according to later reports. Having finished off the potato chips and the champagne, Larwick finally stumbled from the house, which was by now a near total wreck, what with broken glass and the stink of tear gas having ruined much of the interior.

Once they had Larwick safely in custody, the Modesto police realized that they had captured a real-life desperado: Larwick's rap sheet went back more than 20 years; he had a 1976 conviction in nearby Tuolumne County for attempted manslaughter after he'd stabbed a man with a hunting knife, as well as convictions for rape, kidnapping, assault with a deadly weapon, child-stealing, and a number of drug arrests.

Aside from his long criminal past, the most unusual thing about Larwick was his notoriety in rural Tuolumne County as the son of a man, Leroy Larwick, who had created a sensation back in the late 1960s when he claimed to have filmed Bigfoot—the legendary apelike creature said to haunt the woods of the far western mountain ranges. Being the son of the man who claimed to have taken a picture of Bigfoot was Michael Larwick's childhood claim to fame as he was growing up in the small Tuolumne County hamlet called Long Barn; as of the day of Larwick's arrest in Modesto in the early morning hours of March 17, Long Barn was just an unknown bump on the road as far as most poeple were concerned.

But that was about to change.

Four days after the vigil in Modesto, and the day after Larwick surrendered in the Grijalvas' house, a man in a Jeep looking for wood to cut on a remote stretch of Highway 108, just before Long Barn, found himself on an isolated old logging road. Branching off on an overgrown feeder track, the man came upon the reddish-orange, burned-out hulk of a late-model car. One month and four days after Carole, Juli, and Silvina were last seen, the missing 1999 Pontiac Grand Prix had finally been located—far outside the boundaries of Yosemite Park, and more than 100 miles north of El Portal, but within a pistol shot of the very place where Michael Larwick grew up.

Whoever had left the car in this out-of-the-way spot had done a first class-job of torching it; indeed, the first officers at the scene couldn't see a single combustible item on or in the car that hadn't been completely burned.

The woodcutter, Jim Powers of Long Barn, wasn't sure that the car was the one everyone had been talking about for so long, but he realized it was certainly worth a call to the authorities. Soon the California Highway Patrol was on the scene, followed quickly by Tuolumne County Sheriff's deputies, and then the FBI. This was the car everyone had been looking for; that was clear from the rear license plate, whose raised letters and numbers were still discernible despite the scorching that had devoured the paint. The CHP established a roadblock across Highway 108, and deputies strung up yellow crime scene tape for a mile along each side of the road.

Processing an outdoor crime scene, particularly one

in overgrown, densely wooded terrain such as this one near Long Barn, requires special care. First, a perimeter around the scene must be established—preferably, the larger, the better. Next, an assessment must be made as to how the perpetrator made his or her way to the scene, and even more important, how he made his way out.

At least one clue was immediately apparent: the person who left the car on the overgrown rode had driven the vehicle into the woods from Highway 108, had taken the first logging road, and turnèd into the smaller track, only to have the car become hung up on a hump in the middle of the track. There it stuck, unable to go forward or back.

Later, the FBI would be extremely reticent in describing just how the disposer of the car had managed to make it burn so efficiently, although it seems likely that gasoline may have been used to make certain the interior was thoroughly consumed; however it was accomplished, the complete torching had the effect of making it almost impossible to acquire critical forensic evidence, such as hairs, fibers, and fingerprints necessary to link a specific individual to the crime scene; that in turn seemed to show that the perpetrator was both organized and aware of the dangers posed by forensic evidence.

One thing was immediately clear from a cursory inspection of the interior of the car: there were no human remains in either the front or the rear seats of the vehicle.

One of the worst mistakes that can be made in processing a crime scene is moving too fast, trying to do too much, too soon. The longer everything is left in place, the better the opportunity to reconstruct what happened—and correspondingly, to understand the significance of the evidence.

As investigators scoured the site around the car, something unusual was observed: at least one roll of exposed film was found on the ground outside the burned area. The film was taken into custody by the FBI. But a cursory search of the surrounding woods showed no signs of either Carole, Juli, or Silvina.

As the afternoon grew late and the temperatures began to drop, the threat of rain or snow appeared; in the failing light and with the prospect of bad weather, it was decided to secure the scene for another, fresher look the following day.

The word of the discovery of the car spread rapidly on Thursday afternoon, in part due to the curiosity of nearby residents. Several people noticed a gathering of police vehicles in the area in the late afternoon, which was soon augmented by the CHP roadblock and the crime scene tape. One local approached one of the officers and learned of the discovery of the car.

Later the same afternoon, the FBI confirmed the car's discovery with an announcement, but said that so far, no bodies had been recovered. Nick Rossi explained that the car had been burned "in an apparent attempt to conceal evidence."

"Search efforts are underway in the area where the car was recovered," Maddock added. "Most likely the car was placed there by someone who knew the area. It was well-hidden in a very rugged area. I believe this is conclusive evidence of a violent crime—they were either abducted or carjacked. This is not an area . . . somebody stumbles upon."

In Modesto, the reporters rushed to Francis Carrington and Raquel Pelosso for their reactions.

"We're actually elated that they found the car," Francis said. "It's helping us solve the mystery that has befuddled us for the last month. It's a very important step." He said the family would gladly pay the man who had found the car the $50,000 reward that had been promised, and added that a new $50,000 reward would be offered for anyone with information leading to the arrest and conviction of whoever was responsible for the disappearances.

The fact that no bodies were found in or around the car was taken as a hopeful sign by the families.

"We've been told just the car has been found," said Raquel. "They might be somewhere else."

That night, the FBI moved its temporary investigation headquarters from the Doubletree Inn in Modesto to the county seat of Tuolumne County at Sonora, a historic mining town some 20 miles west of Long Barn. The next day, the FBI said, it planned to go over the ground with a painstaking search for any evidence of the fate of the missing trio.

The news of the car's discovery launched another media invasion, this time of the series of small villages along Highway 108 east of Sonora running up to Long

Barn; these included the Gold Rush hamlets of Twain Harte, Confidence, Mi-Wuk Village, Sierra Village, and Long Barn; perhaps because of the new reward offer, the area suddenly seemed awash in new sightings of the missing trio, almost all of which were dutifully recounted by reporters.

Two area business owners, one the operator of a gas station, the other a gift shop proprietor, told of seeing three women visit their establishments on February 16—the day after the last confirmed sighting at Cedar Lodge in El Portal. Just why Carole, Juli, and Silvina would have wandered up Highway 108 toward Long Barn, at an elevation of nearly 5,000 feet and in the opposite direction of their planned stop that day at the University of the Pacific in Stockton, wasn't explained.

The 71-year-old gas station owner, who ran a Chevron station in Sierra Village several miles west of where the car was found, told reporters she was sure she'd sold the missing trio some gas on February 16; one of the girls, she said, had purchased a snack from the station's food store.

"They were in my station," the gas station owner insisted. "I asked her [the girl] if she was heading back home, and she said, 'No, I live in Argentina.'"

The gift shop owner was equally convinced the missing trio had visited her emporium in Twain Harte, a few miles still farther west, and said she'd talked to Carole Sund while the threesome browsed in her store.

Both women said they'd tried to call the FBI hotline in the days following the disappearances; the gas station owner said she'd never been able to get through, so she'd reported the sighting to the Tuolumne County Sheriff's Department, which never followed up. The gift shop owner said she'd twice reached the hotline and had left her number, but that no one had returned her call.

Several of the reporters, probably sensing a "gotcha" sort of story that had the potential of putting the FBI on the defensive, gave both women's accounts credibility without too much skepticism.

The gas station owner claimed that the trio had paid cash for five or six dollars in gasoline before leaving.

"I really felt they were up here all the time," the gas station owner told the *Examiner*'s reporters. "I knew it in my heart. I told everybody that, too. I guess I didn't tell the right person."

The gift shop owner was even more specific about her encounter.

"The mother came in first asking questions about my curtain rods," she told reporters, "and the two girls came in a little later. They were looking at a crystal elephant. They didn't buy anything. They were just browsing. I noticed that they kept looking around the Yosemite area, but everybody saw them up here."

The newspaper treated the two women's accounts as if they were some sort of scoop.

"If the women's accounts are accurate," the *Examiner* reported, "the missing women would have been alive and apparently well later than the previous last known sighting at Cedar Lodge, in El Portal, outside Yosemite National Park. FBI agents have spent hundreds of hours searching for them there, but have found no clues."

Other papers likewise recounted the two women's accounts, backhandedly critizing the authorities for their apparent failure to take the sightings seriously. But the putative sightings would soon collapse under the weight of logic: why would the women be in the area at all? Why would Carole Sund have been interested in the gift shop proprietor's curtain rods? Most especially, why would Carole Sund pay five or six dollars in cash for gasoline when she had a wallet full of credit cards? But those questions would have to be addressed later, because even as the *Examiner* and other papers were rolling over the presses with the two women's dodgy accounts, the FBI's Maddock was making another announcement: two bodies had been found in the trunk of the burned-out wreck.

SIXTEEN

MADDOCK CONDUCTED HIS PRESS conference at Mi-Wuk (once Miwok, for the Yosemite area tribe) Village, just a few miles from where the car was still being processed by investigators. Both of the bodies found in the trunk had been burned beyond recognition, he said.

"The car was very badly burned," Maddock said. "The same is true for the victims [who] were recovered from the car. There is no way to make an identification at this point." Nor, he added, was there any way to say for sure how the victims had died. Maddock said a thorough search of the area was even then underway in an effort to locate a third body in the immediate vicinity.

The car was so badly burned that even the metallic vehicle identification number was obliterated, Maddock said. So was the odometer, as it turned out, which would eventually make it more difficult to reconstruct the actual route of the car from the day it had been rented in San Francisco.

"The car was consumed by fire," Maddock said. "Everything in the car was consumed by fire. That's really all I can tell you."

When pressed about the putative sightings on February 16 in Sierra Village and Twain Harte, Maddock insisted that the last credible sightings of the three women was still at Cedar Lodge in El Portal.

Why hadn't the FBI opened the trunk immediately after the car was discovered? The implication was that the delay in announcing the discovery of the bodies had cruelly raised the hopes of the Sund, Carrington, and Pelosso families, only to crush them a day later. But Maddock wouldn't say why the trunk hadn't been opened first thing; it was pointless to try to describe proper forensic procedures to a crowd of reporters that seemed to be growing increasingly hostile.

When pressed directly about the accounts of the gas station owner and the gift shop operator, Maddock declined to respond.

By this point, several others newspapers, including the *Chronicle* and the *Bee* newspapers of central California, had also talked with the two would-be eyewitnesses, who continued to insist they had seen Carole, Juli, and Silvina a day later than the FBI had so far acknowledged.

"The more I've thought about this," the gift shop owner told the *Chronicle*, "the more I know I'm right."

Meanwhile, yet another woman in Twain Harte

popped up saying, she, too, had seen the trio.

As reporters pressed each of these witnesses for more details of their sightings, more details came forth.

"It was a shiny, sunny day," the gas station owner recalled. "I pumped their gas and got cash for it. It was just before I saw a report of them missing."

The prospect that the threesome had indeed been on Highway 108 a day after the FBI insisted they were last seen prompted another spate of telephone calls to the FBI's hotline, many of them claiming to have seen the trio in the Sonora-Highway 108 area in the middle of February, or even later than that.

The FBI's continued insistence on Cedar Lodge as the last credible sighting notwithstanding, some of the media now used the Highway 108 accounts as the basis for criticism of the Bureau, and by extension, Maddock.

In DID FBI IGNORE KEY LEADS IN CASE?, the *Examiner* used the hoary old headline writer's technique of couching criticism in the form of a seemingly innocent question.

"While authorities embarked on a search for a third missing tourist in the remote, rugged foothills of Tuolumne County," wrote reporter Ray Delgado, "questions have been raised about why the FBI did not follow up on reports that the trio was seen in the area the day after they vanished a month ago."

The FBI's Nick Rossi was forced to admit that the agency did, in fact, receive several tips from people who said they saw Carole, Juli, and Silvina in Tuolumne County after February 15. One call, he said, did come in from the gift shop owner on March 14—the day of the vigil, and almost a month after the trio had supposedly visited her gift shop—and no one had followed up. But Rossi said the authorities had so far received 3,000 tips, some placing the trio hundreds of miles away from Yosemite, in different directions, and on the same days. Other calls from the Twain Harte area included a tip from a psychic who said she had "a feeling" that the women were in the area, and another who claimed to have seen the car in the area as late as March 5. There was no record in the FBI's database of the gas station owner's supposed call, Rossi said.

"It has been impossible, with the volume of tips, to give every one of them personal attention," Rossi said. "Not all of them can be right."

The authorities, he said, had to prioritize calls, and in the absence of any reports putting the trio on Highway 108 in the days *immediately* after the disappearance, tips from the Twain Harte area were given a low priority, especially those which came in far after the event.

While Rossi was trying to explain all this, Michael Larwick, was making an initial appearance in a locked courtroom in Modesto. Rumors had already spread that Larwick had just made the FBI's short list of possible suspects in the Sund/Pelosso case—not least because of his having been raised in the same area where the car had been found.

What was it Maddock had said? That the person who put the burned-out car in its location had to be someone intimately familiar with the area around Long Barn? And wasn't Larwick a convicted rapist and kidnapper who had grown up in Long Barn? When it was learned that the FBI had led a raid on Larwick's apartment in

Modesto on the same day the car had been found, reporters put two halves together to make a story. The locking of the courtroom doors for Larwick's arraignment in the shooting of Modesto Officer Silva only fueled the speculation.

But Judge Susan Siefkin said the barring of the courtroom to the press and the public was inadvertant. Although Larwick's arraignment had been scheduled for 1:30 P.M., it was decided to hurry it up a bit; Siefkin simply hadn't realized the doors to the courtroom were still locked when the hearing was held, she said, and apologized to the suspicious media.

Although Larwick was assigned a lawyer from the public defender's office, his formal arraignment was postponed to give him time to find his own. Modesto County authorities said Larwick would be charged with attempted murder (of Silva, who was shot in the lower abdomen, but recovering in Modesto hospital), assault with a deadly weapon, brandishing a weapon, brandishing a weapon for the purpose of making an escape, being a felon in possession of a firearm, and burglary (to wit, the Grijalvas' house and refrigerator).

In addition to those charges, Larwick also faced outstanding warrants from Tuolumne County for drug possession and several driving offenses. If convicted on any of the felonies, Larwick was in line to go to prison for the rest of his life as a "three-strikes" offender. That indeed may have been the reason he initially fled from Officer Silva's routine traffic stop—with a felony drug warrant out on him, Larwick knew he was about to become a hardtime loser.

Still, there were those who readily linked Larwick's behavior on March 16 with the discovery of the Sund/Pelosso car just two days later in his old stomping grounds of Long Barn.

A Modesto *Bee* columnist, Diane Nelson, took all this into account the day after Larwick's brief, closed-door court appearance.

The newspaper, Nelson wrote, had received nearly *four dozen* telephone calls from readers who wondered why the FBI hadn't landed all over Larwick as the most likely suspect in the Sund/Pelosso case.

Many said they called the paper because the FBI's hotline was always busy—presumably jammed. The callers' theme, Nelson wrote, was consistent: somebody should be putting Larwick under the proverbial bright lights until he squealed.

" 'Is it just my imagination, or are there some connections here?' asked Caller Number Twenty-two," Nelson wrote.

Nelson checked with the Modesto Police Department to see if they were grilling Larwick about the Sund/Pelosso case.

"He's no more a suspect than anyone else with a history of violent crime," a spokesman for the Modesto Police Department told Nelson. Which wasn't saying much, given that under the Bureau's solution-by-induction procedure, nearly everyone in the general vicinity with a history of violent crime was a suspect. But Nelson didn't seem to be buying the department's one-size-fits-all theory.

"You know how they say most killers return to the scene of the crime?" Nelson asked. "Well, here's what's odd to me," and she went on to relate how one caller put the case against Larwick succinctly:

"A few weeks later, last Sunday," the caller told Nelson, "they hold a march for the missing women. And two days after that, a few blocks from the intersection where that student found Carole Sund's wallet, Michael Larwick has a shootout with the police. Over what seems to be a simple traffic violation. Why would he shoot a police officer over that?

"And the day after Larwick ends up in jail, someone finds the women's missing car in the very town where he grew up. They say whoever stashed the car would have to have known the area."

Other callers likewise pointed out what appeared to be a string of coincidences apparently connecting the multiple felon Larwick to the Sund/Pelosso case; a few even claimed that Michael Larwick was bosom buddies with Billy Joe Strange and Darrell Stephens, the two El Portal men who had already been jailed after the FBI began poking into their pasts, although as far as any of the authorities could so far determine, that wasn't the case at all.

Nelson ended her column with an apparent question to one of the callers: why were people calling?

"Maybe we call because we just don't want to stand by," said one woman, a grandmother. "The world is so upside down now, it brings me to tears. We want to help catch who's responsible. Because one thing I know is, killers tend to do it again. And they can get away with it, if the rest of us act like we don't care."

The caller's words would turn out to be quite prophetic.

SEVENTEEN

ON THE DAY NELSON'S "JUST WON-dering" column appeared in the *Bee*, the FBI was ar-ranging to have the burned-out hulk of the Grand Prix transported to a more secure and controlled facility for a more detailed search. The car was winched out of its jammed-up location, loaded on a flatbed truck, covered with a tarp, and trucked off to an airport hangar north of Sonora, where the laboratory mavens—the same sort of people defended so ardently by Maddock a few years before—could take their first sustained crack at trying to find out who or what had done this thing.

The whole operation was done in the snow; begin-ning at about 1:30 A.M. Saturday morning, a storm had come in. By 6:00 A.M., about five inches covered the site. That made further ground searching impossible; no one wanted to unwittingly walk over potential evi-dence while it was covered over.

By midafternoon, the CHP removed its roadblock on Highway 108, although the yellow crime scene tape remained up. A steady stream of cars drove by, each pausing slightly as the occupants rubbernecked to get a glimpse of the place where a horrible crime had been discovered; and others came as well, including a woman who passed out flyers about the August, 1996, disappearance of 20-year-old Michael Madden of Modesto, who vanished while fishing at Sand Bar Flat, about 10 miles away.

"Tell them," the woman said, as she passed out her flyers to reporters, "to look for him, too."

That afternoon, Maddock and the Bureau held still another press conference, primarily to update everyone on what had been done so far and where the investigation was headed.

Did the FBI believe that the location of the burned-out car—miles from El Portal and Modesto—mean that more than one person had to be involved in the crime?

"Yes," Nick Rossi said, "the assumption is that more than one person is involved." And James Maddock added, "We're operating under the assumption this was a very difficult crime for one person to commit."

It did, after all, seem a reasonable assumption. How could one person, acting alone, gain control of three vigorous women? And even more important, how could one person *maintain* control of them for any extended period of time—as would be necessary to move the car for such a long distance—if the victims were still alive? And what about the killer's own transportation? If he or she lived in the Long Barn area, how did they get to El Portal, or even Modesto, for that matter? And if they used their own vehicle to get to the place where the three were first abducted, how did they get back to retrieve their vehicle or vehicles later?

Those questions had bedeviled the investigators from the beginning, and it appeared only reasonable to assume that more than one person was involved. That covered both issues: the control question, as well as the transportation. Indeed, even the thoroughness with which the rental car was torched argued for a well-planned, highly organized operation that involved more than one person.

Meanwhile, still more belated sightings of the trio continued to come in, one from a postmistress in Yosemite Valley itself, who said she thought she'd seen the three in the valley on the morning of February 16, and an attendant at a visitors' center in Sonora who thought she'd seen them on February 17. While the first was possible, the second seemed a nonstarter; what would Carole, Juli, and Silvina have been doing in Sonora on February 17, nearly a full day after they'd missed their rendevous with Jens at San Franscisco International on the night of February 16?

On the same Saturday, March 20, the bodies of the women in the trunk were removed to Sonora, where autopsies were scheduled to take place the following Monday; authorities hoped to be able to identify both by that time. The condition of both bodies was terrible; the fire had damaged them almost beyond reasonable identification; they were so badly burned that it was even difficult to determine their gender. And while authorities had Carole and Juli's dental records, Silvina's had to be retrieved from Argentina. Until those records arrived, no one wanted to hazard a guess as to the identity of any of the bodies; the worst thing that could happen at this stage would be to make a mistake.

The FBI had taken special care to prepare the families, once the trunk had been opened on Friday morning and the grisly discoveries were made. Anticipating the media's reaction to the imminent announcement about the bodies, the FBI on Friday had spirited the Carringtons and the Pelossos out of their Modesto hotel in advance of the announcement. Later, however, both families offered words to the media.

"I said a week or two ago," Carole Carrington told reporters, "that I'd cry when the time came, and the time is now. But we still need your help, because we need to find the animals that did this, because there are terrible people out there and we don't want them to do this to anyone else's daughter and granddaughter."

The Pelossos issued a statement through FBI Chaplain Mark O'Sullivan: "This long ordeal has been very difficult for all the families, and we appreciate you allowing our privacy." The entire nation of Argentina, O'Sullivan added, "has one solid heartbeat for this family."

In Eureka, friends of Jens intercepted reporters' calls to him, and said he was too despondent to talk just then.

Later, Jens released a written statement.

"The senseless waste of these precious lives is so incomprehensible, I can't even begin to understand why it happened," Jens wrote. "They were victims of a devious, calculating criminal who most likely is still in the Yosemite area . . . and so it is with sad irony that not only have we lost what dreams and hopes we had for our teenagers, but we lose just the sort of person today's world most desperately needs."

Chronicle reporters dispatched to Eureka High School, where Juli had been a cheerleader and Silvina had been taking classes, found students and teachers alike stunned at the news about the bodies.

"It's the worst thing that could ever happen to anybody," said one student, a good friend of Juli's since the seventh grade. "How anybody could do this shows they are out of their minds."

The prospect of the trio's deaths hit the entire town hard—not only for Carole's own family, but for all the good works she had contributed in her years in Eureka.

"Carole Sund is one of the most important parents in Eureka city schools," said Tim Scott, the school system's superintendent. "She's just a wonderful, wonderful woman. Our community has been torn apart; our hope for a miracle has obviously faded."

On the following day, the specter of still more post–February 15 sightings was again raised, this time by the *San Francisco Examiner*. In a piece that was equal parts surmise, speculation, and putative eyewitness quotes, the *Examiner*'s Michael Dougan set about trying to recreate the journey the three women might have taken as they left the park.

Dougan claimed that so many people had now claimed to have seen Carole, Juli, and Silvina on February 16 and 17 that the FBI was "taking a second look" at the claims.

Dougan made contact with a private investigator—presumably the one hired by the Sunds in the early stages of the investigation—and the investigator told Dougan that he had discovered credit card slips showing that Carole had made a purchase of food items at Yosemite Lodge on February 16—the day after they were last seen, at least in the FBI's scenario. One possible explanation for the later dating might be that the charge was simply posted the following day; there was simply no way to tell for sure. Nevertheless, the credit card slip dovetailed with the story told by the Yosemite Valley postmistress, whom Dougan identified as Donna Mackie, who claimed she'd sold stamps to the trio at the lodge, also that day. Dougan said he was told that one of the women wanted to purchase enough stamps to send a postcard to Argentina.

Moreover, Dougan claimed to have located a witness in Mariposa, at the visitors' center there, who claimed the trio stopped at the center on February 15 to ask directions to the big trees at Mariposa Grove.

The problem with that, however, was that Carole and the girls had checked into Cedar Lodge in El Portal on Sunday, February 14, and of course, were known to be at the lodge on the evening of Tuesday, February 15. Did it make any sense for the three to drive all the way back to Mariposa on Tuesday to ask for directions to a place they could even more easily have found directions to while in the park on Monday morning?

The most logical explanation, of course, is that Carole and the girls stopped at the visitors' center in Mariposa on Sunday, the fourteenth, and the attendant simply was confused as to the date. Or alternatively: it wasn't Carole, Juli, and Silvina at all, but someone else.

"Agents," Dougan wrote, "must now determine what route the victims used to travel from El Portal to where they were found. If reports of their February 16 presence on the Yosemite Valley floor are accurate, only one route is feasible. But it wouldn't have been easy."

Dougan went on to explain: because of horrific flooding of the Merced River in 1997–1998, a good portion of Highway 140 from El Portal into the park had been washed out, and was under reconstruction. Normally, the road was closed from 8:00 A.M. to 6:00 P.M. daily to give the construction crews the time and space necessary to get the work done. That meant for Carole, Juli, and Silvina to visit the park at all via Highway 140, they had to be through the park entrance before 8:00 A.M.

And, Dougan continued, once in the park, they would either have to stay there until after 6:00 P.M., or take another route out. Because Carole and the girls planned to meet Jens at the San Francisco airport that night, it wouldn't have made sense for them to wait until after 6:00 P.M. to exit the park. Therefore, Dougan reasoned, if the February 16 sightings were accurate, Carole, Juli, and Silvina would have taken Highway 120 up the rim of the valley to Crane Flat and the Big Oak Flat park exit.

Dougan therefore set about trying to locate witnesses who might have seen the trio on February 16 along the

Highway 120 route. In this he was partially successful, although he noted that because it was occasionally snowing on February 16, the Highway 120 route was intermittently under chain control, requiring drivers to carry traction devices. It's unlikely that the rented Grand Prix had such devices, however.

After exiting the park, Dougan theorized, the threesome would have descended to the little hamlets along Highway 120—Buck Meadows, and later, Groveland.

By the time Dougan set about retracing what he thought might be the Sund/Pelosso route, literally thousands of the flyers showing Carole, Juli, and Silvina had been circulated—not only by FBI agents, but by the Polly Klass Foundation, and scores of others. And there can be little doubt that the repeated viewing of those flyers had begun to affect some witnesses' recollectons, if not imaginations. This, of course, is exactly why the police show an array of photos to eyewitnesses, not one single photograph of the suspect; they don't want to taint the witnesses' recollections.

In Buck Meadows, Dougan encountered a motel owner who seemed certain that Juli and Silvina had asked him about renting a room. Apparently unsatisfied with the terms, the pair left after a very short conversation, and got into a car with an older woman. The motel operator was certain this encounter took place around 8:30 or 9:00 P.M. on February 16—well after the time the three were to have met Jens at the San Francisco airport.

Still farther down the road, Dougan encountered yet another motel operator, who was sure that all three women had stayed there for the night. The clue had seemed so promising back in February that Jens Sund himself came to the motel to check it out; unfortunately it turned out the visitors were other people from San Jose.

Dougan continued following Highway 120 to where it merged with Highway 49; Highway 49 paralleled the Sierras in a roughly southeast-northwest direction, and joined with Highway 140 in Mariposa before curving around to the north, through a one-stop-sign town called Coulterville, where it crossed Highway 132 (another east-west connector to the Sierras), and continued north to its merger with Highway 120 near the little town of Moccasin, not far from the site of a San Francisco city power station.

The merged highway then continued north past Lake Don Pedro, created a number of years ago by the damming of the Tuolumne River, and neared New Melones Lake, another similarly dam-created reservoir. At that point, Highway 49 turned into Highway 108, the road to Long Barn.

All in all, a very long trip, over a lot of narrow roads. Just why the meticulous planner Carole would attempt such an excursion on the same day of her planned trip to Stockton and her later rendevous with Jens would be a puzzler of the first order, if indeed that was what happened.

Dougan pressed ahead, eventually coming to Sonora, just slightly north of the junction between Highway 49 and Highway 108. Sonora was the county seat of Tuolumne County, and the new temporary headquarters for Maddock's FBI group, now that the car and the bodies had been found.

At Sonora, Dougan wrote, he encountered a woman named Sonia "Sami" Baxter, who said she had been staffing the Tuolumne County Visitors' Bureau in Sonora on February 17—Wednesday, a full day after the planned trip to Stockton and rendezvous with Jens.

Baxter told him, Dougan wrote, that she was "100 percent certain" that the three people she saw were Carole, Juli, and Silvina. When she complimented the woman she thought was Carole on the girls' appearances, the woman responded that one of the girls wasn't her daughter, but was visiting from Argentina.

Several weeks previously, Baxter continued, she'd been contacted by the private investigator, and told her story then; still later, she'd called the FBI; but no one from the Bureau had bothered to contact her until after the car was discovered.

Well, what was one to make of all these sightings—appearances that were rather entirely inconsistent with Carole Sund as the meticulous, careful planner, always on time, taking routes well-reconnoitered in advance? Certainly the FBI didn't think much of the information—primarily because it was inconsistent with the known facts, and because it all came in so late—after the rewards were posted, after the pictures were so widely distributed, after some of the facts were known. Doubtless most of those who thought they saw Carole, Juli, and Silvina were sincere; it was just that there was nothing to verify their theories.

And as matters would turn out, it appeared they were all completely, utterly wrong.

EIGHTEEN

On the same Sunday, March 21, that Dougan's theory graced the pages of the *Examiner*, the Sund, Pelosso, and Carrington families made a special trip to Long Barn, escorted by the FBI.

There they walked to the place where the car had been found, and conducted a brief, private memorial service. Present were Francis and Carole Carrington, Raquel and Jose Pelosso, Ken Sund, Maddock, Tuolumne County Sheriff Dick Rogers, a representative of the Argentine consulate in Los Angeles, and a pool reporter from the news media.

Jose laid down a vase of flowers and began to weep. Ken Sund did the same. Carole Carrington added water to the flowers.

"Such a glorious spot," Francis Carrington said.

There simply wasn't much else anyone could say.

On the following Monday, March 22, Maddock and his team held a meeting in Sonora with representatives of the Tuolumne and Stanislaus counties Sheriff's Departments and the Modesto Police Department. Now that definitive evidence of a crime had been discovered, Maddock intended to form a joint federal/local task force to unravel the mystery and bring the killers to justice. Fifteen FBI agents would be assigned full-time to the case, along with five Tuolumne County deputies, four Stanislaus County deputies, and two Modesto detectives. The investigation would be called TOURNAP, for tourist kidnapping.

The investigation had made an important transistion: what had begun as a missing persons case, even a possible search-and-rescue situation, had now become a homicide case. The legal jurisdictions remained murky in the absence of facts, however. Who would have responsibility of prosecuting, the locals or the federal government?

It all depended on where the crimes were committed. If the three had been kidnapped or carjacked inside the park, the FBI would have jurisdiction. But if the abduction had taken place in El Portal, arguably the jurisdiction would belong to Mariposa County, where the crime had started. But if people liike Dougan were right, and the trio had made it to either Modesto or Sonora of their own free will, then jurisdiction might belong to either Stanislaus County, where Modesto was county seat, or Tuolumne County, if the crimes had taken place in or near Sonora.

And these were not idle matters: a normally required element of any prosecution is to be able to prove that the alleged crime took place in the jurisdiction where the charges were lodged.

The trouble was, at this point, no one involved with the TOURNAP task force had the answers to any of the legally important questions, let alone to the big one: who did it?

The main thing to focus on at this point, everyone agreed, was to try to assemble as many facts as possible as soon as possible; if everyone cooperated, the jurisdictional issues could be sorted out later when more facts were clear.

On at least one front, Maddock had some news. The FBI had processed the film found near the car; the pictures showed Juli, Silvina, and Carol in the park, and because the frames were time-stamped and dated, it was clear they had been in the park on February 15. Copies of some of the photographs were made to distribute to the news media, in the hope that someone who had been in the park might remember the photo-taking sessions, and thereby provide new leads.

More significantly, a number of the photographs showed Carole, Juli, and Silvina in the Cedar Lodge motel room *after* 6:30 P.M. on February 15. That clearly ruled out the possibility that someone had abducted them as they were on the way back to their room following dinner, as some had theorized; or that something untoward had happened in the restaurant lounge on the night of the disappearance. Moreover, the fact that no photographs were taken *after* February 15 appeared to rule out the possibility that the three were

free on February 16 or 17, as all of the new, probably
false, sightings had suggested.

That same afternoon came more news: one of the
bodies in the trunk was definitely that of Carole Sund;
and while it wasn't immediately possible to tell how
she died, one thing seemed clear—Carole had been in
that trunk for a long time, probably more than a month.

The question that remained was: whose was the
other body in the trunk? Was it Juli or Silvina? Or was
it someone else entirely?

Meanwhile, Michael Larwick continued to remain the
locus of rumors about the Sund/Pelosso case. Agents
seized a silver Corvette that belonged to Larwick for a
new search; and while Maddock and Rossi continued
to decline any comment about the FBI's interest in Larwick in connection with the Sund/Pelosso matter—and
for that matter, to decline comment about Billy Joe
Strange and Darrell Stephens—enough winks and nods
oozed out of the investigation to convince reporters that
the FBI and the rest of the TOURNAP task force was
centering in on their main target.

In switching from the missing persons mode to the
homicide investigation mode, an important change also
transpired in the FBI's relationship with the news media. Before the car and the bodies were found, the Bureau wanted the assistance of the news media, and was
generally accessible and cooperative. But from now on,
in the homicide investigation mode, far less information would be forthcoming. For example, both Maddock and Rossi steadfastly refused to comment on

Larwick, or for that matter, Billy Joe Strange or Darrell
Stephens. Asked repeatedly if any of the three were
suspects in the Sund-Pelosso case, Maddock and Rossi
resolutely declined any comment. Rossi tried to explain
why: the Bureau didn't want to damage the integrity of
its investigation by inappropriately releasing details of
its findings, especially those that might be known only
to the killer; that way the agents could help make certain that any information that might be developed was
genuine, rather than the product of someone's media-
informed imagination; and second, if anyone named as
a suspect turned out to be innocent, suggestions to the
contrary by the task force might be devastating to
someone's reputation or privacy. It seemed indeed that
the Bureau had learned a lesson from the Richard Jewell affair, and perhaps as a result, both Maddock and
Rossi kept quiet about anyone the news media continued to link to the case, no matter how hard the reporters
tried to get them to comment, with one unfortunate
exception. But that was to come much later.

Several dozen searchers spent much of Monday,
March 22, scouring the ground around the place where
the car had been found. The snow had melted, and now
the searchers recovered a large number of items that
had apparently once been in the car—clothing and
other personal items that clearly had belonged to Carole, Juli, or Silvina. Assisted by six dogs, the searchers
combed nearly a full square mile for possible evidence.

The information about the FBI's search of Larwick's
apartment naturally prompted speculation that the FBI
believed that he had something to do with the crime—

after all, Larwick's beef was with the Modesto police, so why else would the FBI be searching his belongings? But still Maddock refused to say a word about Larwick.

"We have not arrested anybody in connection with this crime," was all Maddock would say.

Meanwhile, the reported sightings of Carole, Juli, and Silvina near Long Barn continued to come in. Here, the FBI was in a tricky position: they didn't want to cut anyone off, especially someone who might have important information; on the other hand, it was becoming increasingly clear that many of the reported sightings of the trio were simply wrong. The best thing to do, it was decided, was to thank people for taking an interest, and encourage those who had information to continue to call, but make it clear that the most likely time the three had last been seen was still at El Portal.

Francis Carrington threw in some assistance in that regard.

"People have the best intentions in the world," he said, "but I believe these sightings [near Long Barn] were invalid." His daughter, Francis said, was simply too organized and meticulous to have headed off on an unplanned jaunt in the direction of Long Barn.

Even as Francis Carrington was making the point that the crime had probably begun near Yosemite, experts were poring over the burned-out hulk of the Grand Prix at the nearby airport hangar. Even with the conflagration, some experts said, it might still be possible to develop important forensic evidence from the car. Floorboards might be a valuable repository for such evidence as hairs and fibers, primarily because fire tends to burn upward, leaving the lower layers relatively unscathed. Some experts even suggested that recovery of fingerprints from the car might be possible, especially with new types of chemical substances available to the FBI.

But these theories came from those who hadn't actually seen the car; so badly burned was it that it was unlikely to yield any useable fingerprints. That appeared to be borne out by the fact that in the days after the car's recovery, no one was rushing out to put the cuffs on any obvious culprits.

And there was the final question: whatever had become of the third victim? The searchers had scoured the ground around the car, even looked for shallow graves, but nothing could be found. No one knew whether it was Juli or Silvina in the car; neither teenager's dental records was sufficient to identify the second body. That meant efforts had to be made to use DNA evidence for the identification, always a chancy proposition when a victim's remains have been badly damaged in a fire. So here was yet another torture for the Sunds, Carringtons, and Pelossos: who was it in the trunk with Carole? Was it Juli? Was it Silvina? And if it was one, whatever had become of the other? Was she still alive someplace, hoping for rescue? It was almost too much to contemplate, more than a month into the ordeal.

NINETEEN

WITH THE TASK FORCE ENTERING
its investigative mode, and sources beginning to clam
up, the news media did what it usually does in such
situations: it sums up.

Thus, both San Francisco newspapers, as well as the
Bees in Fresno, Modesto, and Sacramento, all published roundup pieces on the investigation so far; and
each suggested that the TOURNAP task force was working on the theory that the three women were the random victims of a crime of opportunity probably
perpetrated by some group of lowlifes who hung out
in the Sierra foothills. Prominently featured, although
not by name in every case, was Michael Larwick,
whose lurid past as an attempted murderer, rapist, violent assaulter, kidnapper and drug user were high-
lighted. Neither Billy Joe Strange nor Darrell Stephens
was mentioned by name, but they were accounted for,
the papers left no doubt.

"Although they won't acknowledge it, FBI and other

investigators are known to be looking at three men whose identities are widely known in the Mother Lode area as possible suspects," the *Examiner* reported on March 24. The *Chronicle* gave forth in a similar vein on the same day.

"The prime thrust of the probe," the newspaper reported, "is now questioning ex-cons and parolees from the thickly wooded Sierra to the Central Valley and working forensics on materials taken from the car scene and from the homes and vehicles of potential suspects. And although FBI agents are not tipping their hand, they say they have many viable leads that are narrowing their search."

The *Chronicle* next sketched in a rather sinister atmosphere it said underlay the whole case: while most people thought of the Gold Rush country as a scenic, rustic playground of forests, historic villages and ski resorts, there was a hidden underside to the area, the paper contended.

"But there is a dark vein beneath the glitter of the gold country, a world hiding rough mountain men, clandestine drug labs, and felons," the *Chronicle* continued, making the task force members sound like miners. "And it is in that vein that investigators are digging deep."

Off side roads leading away from both Highway 140 and Highway 108, the paper reported, were little-noticed dirt roads leading to isolated cabins, often without telephones or electricity, where people did pretty much as they pleased, with nobody to see them, or even care.

"Methamphetamine labs abound, as do parolees, and other ex-cons," the *Chronicle* asserted.

Articles of a similar type ran in other newspapers, as well; and it wasn't long before the tone was picked up by the broadcast media, too. The message: the woods around El Portal, Long Barn, and similar Sierra foothill communities were filled with real and potential criminals, many of whom knew one another, and many of whom were as capable of cutting someone's throat as forget to pay their income taxes. These were the sort of people the task force believed had committed the Sund/Pelosso crimes.

"The areas around El Portal and Long Barn are full of them, and that's part of the trouble," one unnamed investigator told *Chronicle* reporters. "There are too many people capable of this kind of crime. It's hard to narrow it down."

And the same was true around the bigger city of Modesto, the newspaper added. For several weeks, the paper said, authorities had staked out houses of parolees and known drug users living in the city. In fact, the paper said, the task force was looking intensively at about 10 different, loosely connected parolees and ex-cons, most living in the Long Barn, El Portal, and Modesto areas. The very fact that the task force was interested in the 10 people suggested on the surface that someone in authority believed that one, or more likely more, might be involved in the Sund/Pelosso abductions.

The fact that all three newspaper establishments ran the same sort of story the same week could hardly have

been a coincidence; in retrospect, it appears that someone was attempting to prepare the public for the effort
that was to follow. The Modesto *Bee*, at least, attempted to pin the FBI down on what it was up to, but
Nick Rossi deftly deflected the inquiry.

"There's always a balance in an investigation between what you can make public and what you can't,"
Rossi said. "The balance shifts sometimes, especially
when you have to make a public appeal for assistance.

"The fact remains there are some pieces of information known only to us and to those who were involved. It's necessary to keep that kind of information
secret."

By the middle of the week it was no longer any
secret what the TOURNAP task force was up to: it was
busy rousting every parolee, probationer, and ex-con in
the three counties. It didn't much matter who was doing
what; if someone had a record, there was a man with
a badge questioning them.

The whole thing was making a lot of people nervous,
the *Examiner* reported.

"It's great," said the gas station owner who'd been
so sure she'd sold $5 or $6 in gas to Carole Sund the
week before. "They're driving away everybody with a
criminal record. I don't know if they're going to find
the person they want up here, but they're making all
the bad guys nervous."

The *Examiner* confirmed the *Chronicle*'s assertion
that the authorities had targeted a loosely associated
group of parolees in connection with the investigation,

but said it had learned the group of bad guys could be as large as 15.

It was, said Tuolumne County Sheriff's Lieutenant John Steely, merely routine. Investigators were only checking alibis of those with known criminal records, he insisted.

The heavy sweep was applauded by several residents of both Mariposa and Tuolumne counties as long overdue. The *Examiner* checked with the state's Department of Corrections, and learned that Tuolumne County had 115 parolees and 95 registered sex offenders; Mariposa had only 20 parolees and 42 registered sex offenders. That figure was down from the 55 reported the year before, so it appeared that at least some registered sex offenders had departed before the roust was on.

But the papers barely had time to digest the meaning of the Great Parolee Sweep of 1999 (which had begun so modestly with Billy Joe Strange and Darrell Stephens only three weeks before) when another significant event intervened.

TWENTY

IT WAS WHILE ALL THE PAPERS were predicting the imminence of the great parolee roundup on Wednesday, March 24, that the anonymous letter mailed 10 days earlier finally arrived at its intended destination; and while the text of the letter wasn't made public, it was immediately clear that the writer was someone who almost certainly knew whatever had happened to Carole, Juli, and Silvina.

In addition to taunting the FBI for its failures so far, and boasting of his or her own prowess, the writer suggested that the authorities look for Juli's body near Highway 49 near Lake Don Pedro. In fact, the letter was quite specific as to where Juli's body might be found: near a scenic overlook not far from Moccasin Point.

The psychological experts examined the letter forward and backward, and at length pronounced it a probably genuine article.

The following day, even as the *Examiner, Chronicle,*

and the *Bee* were predicting the big parolee roust, a team from the task force, assisted by the Tuolumne County Sheriff's Department and the California Highway Patrol, went to the scenic overlook. There, stuffed in a patch of poison oak about 100 yards away from where tourists often stopped to snap pictures of the lake and the mountains, was the body of 15-year-old Juli Sund.

It was immediately obvious that Juli's body had been at the location for quite some time—probably at least a month, if not more. Found down inside a steep, grassy ravine that overlooked the waters of the lake, it was less than 100 yards from a historical marker commemorating the Gold Rush town of Jacksonville. Juli's hands were crossed over her chest, and her ankles were lashed together with duct tape, facts that were not released to the news media. Nor was the apparent cause of death: a deep cut to the neck, one that nearly severed her head from the rest of her body. After so many weeks, the body was in a state of severe decomposition.

The task force refused to say how or why it had discovered Juli's body; the fact that the anonymous letter had given such explicit directions would remain one of the task force's secrets for months to come.

And yet the location was significant; it was rapidly observed that the site was midway between El Portal and Long Barn; that someone who had driven back down Highway 140 to Mariposa, then north on Highway 49 would have passed the scenic overlook and historic marker; and while no one in the press made mention of it, the fact that there was only a single stop sign all the way from Mariposa to the site, and that one in the tiny crossroads of Coulterville, would have made the Highway 49 route almost ideal for someone who didn't wish to be disturbed while driving. To some that single fact seemed to eliminate Highway 120 as the route to the killing ground.

Likewise, it appeared from forensic evidence available around the body in the ravine that the killer had dispatched Juli on the spot; in turn, that meant that somehow she had been kept alive for hours, if not days, following the February 15 disappearance.

And there was more: if the killer had left El Portal with a living Juli, where were Carole and Silvina while he was driving? Again this was an argument for more than one killer: two or more killers in the red car, and perhaps a third following behind with backup transportation. The other alternative was that the killer or killers had murdered Carole and Silvina first, near El Portal, and deposited their bodies in the trunk, later driving Juli to the lake for her last seconds of life. After having left Juli dead at the lake, the killer or killers would have continued up Highway 49 to the Highway 108 junction, then to Long Barn, where the car would have been torched with Carole and Silvina's bodies in the trunk.

But that still left the question: how did the killer or killers get away from Long Barn? Or, if they lived near Long Barn, how did they get to El Portal? Either way, the solution required at least a second vehicle; and it was in this area that the task force's largest assumption was to prove its biggest error.

And finally, there was the question: why was Juli left at the lake, while Carole and Silvina were taken so many miles away and left under entirely different circumstances? Profilers have long argued that random killers—and surely that was what had happened to the Sund-Pelosso victims—continue to replicate their method of killing: one, because it fulfills a peculiar fantasy each individual might have, and second, because they feel safer by avoiding variances.

But the scene for Juli was totally different than that of Carole and Silvina; in turn, that led some behavioral experts to argue that two different killers were involved.

And while the pyschologists were at it, there were two other questions: what was the significance of the lake—or perhaps the historic marker delineating the town of Jacksonville—and what, if any, was the significance of Long Barn? Two more different environments could hardly be imagined. Was there some message in the selection of the sites for the disposal of the bodies? If so, it wasn't readily apparent; this once more provided support for the notion of more than one killer: one with a preference for the lake, another with a preference for the higher mountains.

And in any case, the use of Highway 49 only reinforced the notion that had so long abided in the minds of the investigators: whoever had victimized Carole, Juli, and Silvina, he or she was almost certainly a local person, someone intimately familiar with the region's roadways. A tourist from the city would never have picked either of those locations to get rid of bodies;

indeed, there were ten thousand locations between El Portal and Modesto where a car with three bodies might be hidden and never found. It was only the fact that someone had sent the anonymous letter that led the authorities to Juli's body; if it hadn't been for that, she might never have been found.

Which in itself prompted something of a heretical idea in some investigators' minds: was the taunting letter a message from someone no one had yet thought of as a suspect—someone so far out of the loop as to be offended that he or she wasn't being taken seriously? Was the task force galloping off in the wrong direction completely with the parolees?

It just didn't seem very likely. The murders showed all the signs of more than one person involved; moreover, they were cleverly perpetrated, covering a wide span of territory, down to and including Modesto. Clearly, most investigators thought, this was an organized killing spree, and almost certainly beyond the capacity of a single individual.

The remains of Juli Sund were quickly identified from dental records early the following morning, March 26; Tuolumne County Sheriff Dick Rogers said the identification almost certainly meant that the second body in the trunk at Long Barn was that of Silvina Pelosso, although final positive identification would require DNA tests that could only be done by the FBI lab on the East Coast.

Both Rogers and Maddock, at a press conference that afternoon, swore to get the killers, and suggested that a great volume of forensic evidence such as hairs and fibers from the crime scenes were even then being examined at the FBI's laboratory.

"The investigation is proceeding at an intensified rate," Rogers said.

But Rogers didn't say how intensified; even as he and Maddock were briefing reporters, the Great Parolee Sweep of 1999 had finally cranked into high gear. By the end of the day, at least ten different men, mostly in Modesto, had been swept up by raiding law enforcement officers and packed off to the Stanislaus Public Safety Center near Ceres, California. In addition, at least 15 stolen cars were recovered in Tuolumne and Mariposa counties, according to the *Examiner*. The task force was bringing the heat, and it would not be too long before all sorts of tales would come spilling out of the violatees, some of them even true.

One of the first to go down was a six-foot, five-inch, 41-year-old former sex offender, Larry Utley, long believed by police to be associated with the methamphetamine trade. Officers pulled him out of a friend's house early on the morning of March 26 and charged him with failing to register as a sex offender and on possession of drugs. After about 12 hours in jail, Utley made bail and was released, but it wouldn't be the last the law heard of him.

Still another man, 32-year-old Jeff Keeney, was nabbed in a Turlock, California, residential neighborhood after a brief car and foot chase and charged with parole violations. Pursuing officers found a trail of illegal drugs left behind that they said Keeney had thrown from his pockets while being pursued. Because of the drugs, the officers went to a nearby house where Keeney had been living and claimed to have discovered three methamphetamine labs, boxed and ready for transport. While the cops were busy with the boxes, another man walked in, and was also arrested.

It also developed that still another man, 32-year-old Eugene Earl "Rufus" Dykes—Michael Larwick's half-brother—had been arrested for parole violations in southeast Modesto on March 5, the same day that Billy Joe Strange was taken into custody. In a twist, Rufus was sent back to prison on the same day that his older half-brother, Larwick got into the shootout with Modesto officer Silva.

As the task force looked into these and other Modesto area men, they began to believe that most of them knew one another, and that they sometimes did business with each other. The notion of a loose-knit gang of methamphetamine makers, dealers, and users somehow being involved in the Sund-Pelosso case began to gain even more plausibility.

"Interviews with numerous law enforcement sources and others who are close to the case," the *Chronicle* reported on Saturday, March 27, "reveal that the investigation has zeroed in on a loosely formed crowd of ex-convicts and parolees who, when they are not behind bars, live in the rugged country that forms the lower foothills of the gold country.

"In addition to convictions for narcotics violations and other crimes, violence against women is a constant that runs through many of their criminal histories."

On the same day, the Modesto *Bee* described the parolee roundup, and contended that the FBI had ordered the arrests to grill the parolees about possible involvement in the murders.

"Although no one has been identified as a suspect," the *Bee* reported, "FBI agents continue to question Eugene Burel Dykes, the father of Larwick's half-brother, Dykes told the *Bee*." The senior Dykes was also a former convict, he would later acknowledge.

Even Larwick's father—the man who once claimed to have filmed Bigfoot up near Long Barn—was caught up in the drama.

"I don't want to get involved in anything right now," he told the *Bee*. "I'm very unhappy with him [Michael Larwick] and the whole situation."

The next day, Sunday, March 28, the *Bee*'s Michael Mooney summed up the events, and sounded as if he'd been reading the same playbook as the *Chronicle* and the *Examiner*:

"One theory investigators are said to be exploring is the possibility that those who killed the sightseers are associated with a loosely knit collection of rogue ex-cons and parolees who move between the foothills and the valley." After having named Utley, Keeney, Michael Larwick, and "Rufus" Dykes the day before, Mooney rounded out the rogue's list by mentioning Billy Joe Strange and Darrell Stephens, still cooling their heels in the Mariposa jail.

Thus, by the end of March, the theme was pretty well set: while no one was saying officially that the killers of Carole, Juli, and Silvina were the "loose-knit rogue ex-cons and parolees" who flitted between hills and valley, the fact that the FBI seemed so interested in all of them had to mean something.

Didn't it?

TWENTY-ONE

APRIL WAS FOR FUNERAL SERVICES.
First was a private graveside ceremony for Juli attended
by Jens and his family at St. Bernard's Cemetery in
Eureka; Carole's body was still being held by the FBI
for further forensic tests. The next day, Sunday, April
11, a large, community-wide service was held in Eureka at Sacred Heart Church, where more than 1,000
people attended in remembrance of Carole and Juli.
Among the attendees was California Senator Dianne
Feinstein.

As the service began, the sun broke through the of-
ten cloudy Eureka skies; ushers handed out daisies,
Juli's favorite flower; posters of Juli leading cheers at
Eureka High School were placed on easels around the
church, and bouquets of flowers were placed next to
Juli's violin; she'd played in the high school orchestra.
Carole's gardening hat and trowel were placed on a
nearby table to symbolize her love for her garden.

Opening the memorial service, Monsignor Thomas

Keys prayed for the healing of the Sund and Carrington families, and called upon the trio's killers to come forward to be held accountable.

"Free this family," Keys said. "Come forward so they can put this terrible tragedy to rest."

Although the service was organized as a celebration of Carole and Juli's lives, a note of anger and vengeance soon crept in.

The moderator of the service, Ron Caton, Jens Sund's brother-in-law, told the crowd that he hoped the deaths of the trio would spur political officials to pass tougher laws designed to keep violent felons locked up.

"We don't want them to have a second or a third chance to commit violent crimes," Caton said. Even the state's "three strikes law" (in which three-time convicted felons get 25 years to life in prison) was too lenient, in Caton's view. "Ladies and gentlemen, I say to you emphatically: three strikes are too many."

Ken Sund said he'd already talked with several state political leaders about tightening laws to keep violent criminal behind bars longer.

Senator Feinstein was somewhat on the spot. As an elected official, she was one of those who was partially responsible for enacting laws such as those proposed by Ken Sund and Ron Caton. But Feinstein wasn't about to commit herself to some vague campaign to crank up the terms of criminal punishment, despite the circumstances of attending a memorial service for two innocent crime victims.

The first thing to do, she said, was let the FBI find

out who was responsible, and whether they were repeat offenders.

"Let's see what happened," Feinstein said. "Let's see who the perpetrators turn out to be, and if they're caught, what their background is, and then you can make some judgments."

Carole Sund was praised over and over for her commitment to helping troubled children—exactly the sort of people who often turn into criminal defendants. The irony of her death at the hands of someone so much like those she tried to help was lost on no one.

Yet another memorial service was held for the trio in Modesto on the following night; in a way, it was amazing: a town that had never heard of the Sunds until that horrible day in February turned out to bid them good-bye. Many of those in attendance had volunteered their time to work on the Sund and Carrington families' behalf during the long, excruciating days in February and March before the three victims were finally located.

"What a wonderful town," said Francis Carrington. "Thanks a lot. I hope we will be seeing you again."

One person other people were seeing was Michael Larwick. On the first of April, the Long Barn man granted an interview to a Fresno television reporter. Larwick said FBI agents had questioned him for 16 hours about the Sund-Pelosso case, but he had insisted throughout that he had nothing to do with the crimes. He said he'd provided a blood sample to the investigators for a DNA comparison.

Not only did he not have anything to do with the murders, Larwick continued, he'd never met Billy Joe Strange or Darrell Stephens and didn't know them at all.

And in another interview, this one with the Modesto *Bee*, Jeff Keeney also denied involvement with the crimes.

"I had nothing to do with it," Keeney said. "I have no idea why they connected me with that. I've done a lot of things . . . I could never do something like that. My morals are good, you know what I mean? I was brought up right."

He'd taken a polygraph test, Keeney said, and passed; in addition, he'd given hair samples. Together, he said, that evidence would clear him of involvement with the murders.

Not only that, Keeney continued, he wasn't even a friend of Larwick, although he might have met him once or twice while both were in prison. He said he was grateful for his family's support, especially his wife, despite his recent difficulties.

"I'd like to thank the women in my life," Keeney said, "for believing in me. It makes a difference. I love every one of them."

Meanwhile, back in Mariposa, Darrell Stephens was being bound over for trial on his failure to register as a sex offender. Like Larwick and Keeney, Stephens, through his attorney, denied any involvement in the Sund-Pelosso murders. In fact, said Stephens's lawyer, the best thing that could happen to Stephens would be for the FBI to solve the case; that would show that Stephens had nothing to do with it.

But if Larwick, Keeney, and Stephens were adamantly denying any involvement in the murders, it was a whole different story from Michael Larwick's half-brother, Eugene "Rufus" Dykes.

The term, of course, is stir crazy; that's what happens in stir. The walls close in, the real world recedes, the time gets hard. Some people will do anything in prison to get some excitement, something new to keep them entertained. Perhaps the classic case of confession-as-entertainment is that of Henry Lee Lucas, who once claimed to have committed nearly 100 murders; as detectives from across the country beat a path to Lucas's cell door to hear him confess to all manner of crimes he never committed, Henry was hugely entertained, given special prison privileges, and provided with seemingly endless supplies of tobacco and candy by eager investigators. In the end, however, Lucas recanted all of his admissions; in fact, he claimed, he'd only killed one person in his whole life, and that was his mother.

In any event, early in April, Rufus made contact with the federal investigators. And whatever his motives for talking—and they seemed to vary with the day of the week—once Rufus began to talk, he didn't seem to be able to stop.

Initially, Rufus told the investigators that his half-brother, Larwick, had admitted taking part in the kidnappings; moreover, Rufus said, Michael had given him jewelry from the victims, including checks from Carole Sund's checkbook, and a ring. A female friend, he said, was asked to forge identification in Carole's name to permit access to Carole's accounts. Still another person, Rufus claimed, had taken Carole's wallet to Modesto to dispose of it, to throw the police off the track.

This last hardly seemed likely; why in the world would the "rogue gang" led by Larwick dump Carole's wallet in Larwick's own town? Even the dumbest rogue would have had the sense to dump it some place far away—like San Francisco, or Stockton.

The investigators asked Rufus to take a polygraph test. He did, and the results seemed to show he was being deceptive when he was asked whether he had harmed Silvina.

Their appetite whetted by the apparent deception, the investigators began to suspect that Rufus had been more than just the receiver of confessions and stolen property. One of Rufus's girlfriends was set up by an acquaintance of Rufus. In a monitored conversation, the girl said that Rufus had admitted that he and a second man had killed the three women by slitting their throats.

The slitting of throats assertion captured the investigators' full attention; after all, nothing had been disseminated about the way Juli Sund had died.

As April progressed, investigators began to feel more and more certain that the two half-brothers were at the center of the mystery; as a result, they increasingly focused their attention on trying to find evidence necessary to nail the case down permanently.

*　　*　　*

At least some of the impetus for Rufus's tales appeared to have come from the fact that a federal grand jury had been impaneled in Fresno to hear evidence in the Sund-Pelosso case. Even if the cases were to be eventually prosecuted by state authorities, information developed by a federal grand jury could be used in a state prosecution. By the middle of April, a number of witnesses had testified before the jury, including women friends of Larwick, Keeney, Utley, and Rufus. Utley himself had testified, as did a retired Modesto police officer who currently worked in security for the Modesto *Bee*, who claimed to have developed information from sources that seemed to implicate Michael Larwick in the crimes.

Judging from their demeanor, federal officials were pleased at the progress being made in unraveling the case. The general theory about the "rogue ex-cons" really did seem to be holding up.

On Thursday, April 22, the Modesto *Bee*'s Michael Mooney wrote a rather interesting article about the investigation and its progress so far. The article was prefaced by an unusual note from the *Bee*'s executive editor, Mark S. Vasche; in the note, Vasche acknowledged that it wasn't the *Bee*'s general policy to use news from anonymous sources.

"We know," Vasche wrote, "that a story's—and a paper's—credibility can be undermined by reliance on unnamed sources."

This indeed was a refreshing attitude in current American journalism; there was a time, perhaps 30 years ago, when most newspapers simply refused to use stories that quoted anonymous sources. But as the communications business speeded up over the following decades, more and more news outlets relied ever more heavily on people who wouldn't be quoted by name. The *Chronicle* and the *Examiner*, for example, repeatedly used "sources close to the investigation" as the provenance for information used in their stories on the Sund-Pelosso case.

The trouble with relying on such sources—one often suffered by electronic news outlets even more than print media—is that those who don't want their names used have no real incentive to be truthful; instead, if they can't be caught publicly in a lie (or a "spin," as the current terminology has it), they have every incentive to twist information, either by outright misrepresentation, or more frequently by omission, in order to advance a particular point of view.

Such was the state of play in the Sund-Pelosso case as the spring of 1999 wore on: the widely accepted idea that the murders were the work of the "rogue ex-cons" typified by Larwick and Rufus Dykes took deep root in virtually all the news media outlets, and there it remained until events overtook it.

Mooney's piece—the *Bee*'s exception to its usual policy—was remarkable for its contentions. And although Vasche contended that its assertions had been checked "by another source or method," and that its origins had come from people who were in a position to know the facts, there was all too little in the story that could be independently verified on the record.

"Investigators," Mooney wrote, "are making significant progress piecing together what happened to the three slain Yosemite sightseers. The unfolding scenario, in the words of one law officer, 'makes me sick to my stomach.' "

After cautioning that charges might be weeks away, Mooney dropped in a blind quote—that is, a quote from an unnamed source.

" 'For the first time,' [since the sightseers disappeared], said a source close to the investigation, 'things are finally starting to click.' "

At that point Mooney undercut his own piece substantially by calling it "one possible scenario."

Investigators were chasing down the theory, Mooney continued, that while Carole and Silvina were killed within hours after they disappeared, Juli Sund "is said to have been kept alive for a number of days by her tormentors, who raped the girl repeatedly before killing her."

The source of this rather lurid "scenario," appeared to be thirdhand; in other words, Mooney talked to "someone close to the investigation," who in turn had talked with someone who had told him something he or she had heard about.

In law, this is triple hearsay, and to be avoided like the plague as notoriously unreliable, only a step removed from gossip.

Mooney went on to contend that his unnamed sources told him that "a young Modesto girl . . . reportedly saw Juli Sund in the Modesto area with two men after the trio's disappearance."

The girl, Mooney said his sources told him, "reportedly" told investigators that "the two men bragged to her about what they had done to the women." Moreover, Mooney continued, his sources told him the girl claimed that she'd been given jewelry that had belonged to the victims. Mooney also noted that the girl had said she'd been using methamphetamine when she was told this tale; that was a further strike against the girl's credibility.

"Maddock has refused to elaborate," Mooney reported. "But one source told the *Bee* that investigators are pursuing a theory that Carole Sund was accosted as she left the restaurant by someone who planned to rob her. A short time later, the two girls left the restaurant and happened upon the robbery."

If the investigators cited by Mooney were members of the TOURNAP task force, they surely must have been napping through Maddock's briefings. After all, virtually all of the witnesses in the restaurant agree that the three left the restaurant together; moreover, the unpublished photographs found in the Sund-Pelosso film showed all three women together, and apparently happy and healthy in their motel room well after the dinner hour. So if Mooney's sources were pursuing this accosting idea as a theory, they were certainly climbing the wrong tree. Moreover, Mooney's sources told him they believed that the abduction arose from panic by the would-be robbers after the two girls "happened" upon the attack on Carole on her way from the restaurant. That, of course, was demonstrably untrue, as the photographs showed.

But any time an unnamed source floats a "scenario"

in the news media, one should be well-advised to examine the proferred tale closely for motives. In the case of Mooney's article, the motive was apparent: to again link the "rogue ex-cons," i.e., Larwick, Dykes, and Keeney to the crimes. This is called front-end loading, or even jury-tainting, and is sufficient in a court of law for a judge to issue a finding of prosecutorial misconduct. The fact that the "scenario" was at best unproven and at worst completely wrong made it even more egregious. But that's the advantage taken by "unnamed sources," and delivered at the peril of the journalist as well as his or her public.

Not to be outdone by Mooney, the *Chronicle* whipped together a similar smorgasbord of rumors and gossip, most of which could not be verified. In their story, published Monday, May 10, reporter Stacy Finz assembled a grab bag of the possible, the likely, the rumored, and the unprovable in a sort of Felliniesque tour of TOUR-NAP to date.

At least the *Chronicle* headline writer got the tone right: YOSEMITE SLAYING PROBE HURT BY LIES, RUMORS, ODDBALLS, it read.

Finz noted that ever since the federal grand jury began its work, "a stream of oddball witnesses ranging from jail inmates to known drug dealers have been paraded" before the jurors.

"And while authorities have narrowed their focus on two half-brothers they think may have been involved, they have had mixed success in getting people to tell them what really happened."

Finz went to the FBI's Nick Rossi to put the circus into perspective:

"There have been a lot of rumors circulating on this case, ranging from the cause of death to speculation about particular pieces of evidence, that have turned out to be untrue," Rossi said.

With that, Finz went on to establish "what the FBI does know," citing "sources close to the case."

More than two people were involved in the crimes and the coverup, Finz asserted; both Larwick and Rufus Dykes "may have been involved"; the abductions occurred in "either Mariposa or Tuolumne counties;" and "Juli may have been separated from the two and kept alive longer."

Finz discussed some of the witnesses who had so far testified before the grand jury, but noted that "their information is not always reliable."

As an example, Finz pointed to the tale previously recounted by Mooney about Juli being held captive in a Modesto house. "Authorities hold little stock in the information, but are checking it out just the same," Finz reported.

One tale making the rounds was that some of Larwick and Dykes's women friends had been seen wearing jewelry that belonged to Carole Sund, including Carole's wedding ring, Finz said. But the fact was, Carole hadn't worn the wedding ring on the trip, according to Jens, Finz reported. This seemed to be a variation on the ring story told earlier by Mooney.

And there was also a tale that a 36-year-old Modesto woman, an acquaintance of Larwick and Dykes in jail

on unrelated charges, had somehow come into possession of Carole's checking account and ATM numbers.
Just how that could have happened when Carole's wallet was recovered intact was a mystery; it was, of
course, possible that the killers had written the numbers
down before disposing of the wallet, but there was no
proof that anyone unauthorized had ever accessed Carole's account.

And there were others who had momentarily wandered across the stage: a Salida man, said to have specialized in making counterfeit mailbox keys, was found
drowned in early April; his relatives claimed that he
had witnessed Juli Sund being assaulted in the Modesto
house, and that because of this, he had been murdered;
the fact that this story surfaced two weeks after Mooney's "sources' scenario" did little to improve its
credibility.

And finally there was a man who told the FBI that
he had an audiotape of a witness who had a lot of
information about the murders.

"But instead of giving the tape to investigators, the
man sold it to a television tabloid show," Finz reported.

Finz gave the bottom line back to the federals:
"We're not dealing with the most upstanding people
here. But we have to do what we can with it."

TWENTY-TWO

By mid-May, in the absence of anything official from the FBI's TOURNAP task force, the hodgepodge of media rumors from "sources close to the investigation" had begun to abate. In one of his increasingly rare interviews, James Maddock told a reporter for the *Examiner* that he was "100 percent confident" that the case would be solved.

"I can say that we've made remarkable progress," Maddock told *Examiner* reporter Ray Delgado. "We are on the right track . . . it won't be long [before] we'll be in a position to charge those responsible for the deaths."

Maddock may have been "100 percent confident" that a solution to the case was on the horizon, but even he knew there was still a substantial amount of routine investigative work that remained to be undertaken. One task that had to be done was to reinterview all the members of the Cedar Lodge staff, this time with the idea of developing information that might link one or more of the Modesto targets of the investigation to the El Portal area or the lodge itself.

As part of this routine, agents found themselves once more talking with Cary Stayner. At some point during this interview, Cary was asked where he had actually been the night Carole, Juli, and Silvina had last been seen; Cary said he'd been visiting a woman friend in El Portal. Agents checked with the woman, and confirmed that indeed, Cary had been with her on the night of February 15. Similar inquiries were made of others, yet nothing seemed to jump out to investigators as anything close to a smoking gun to link the rogues to the abduction.

By late May, however, the TOURNAP agents had received a report on some potentially important forensic evidence from the lab. It appeared that some pink fibers found on and near the body of Juli Sund had also been collected from a Jeep occasionally used by Rufus Dykes, from a pickup truck owned by a friend of Rufus, and from Larwick's impounded Corvette. The same sort of fibers were found on Dykes's jacket. Similarly, there were other fibers, perhaps from Juli's clothing, that were found in the vehicles.

Fiber evidence has long been considered one of the most potent tools of the FBI lab. The vast profusion of different types of fibers, both natural and synthetic, in recent years, along with their vast array of colors, had made it possible to distinguish types of fibers with a high degree of specificity, far more than hair types. Even more significantly, tiny fibers and fiber fragments are frequently transferred when two objects come into contact. The tiny pink fibers appeared to come from some sort of blanket; the theory was developed that perhaps one or more of the victims had been wrapped in a pink blanket during the transportation process, which would account for how the fibers appeared on and near Juli, and also in Dykes's and Larwick's cars and on Dykes's jacket.

The question was: was there a similar blanket available at Cedar Lodge? Was that where the pink fibers had originally come from?

Agents approached the lodge management and asked for permission to search the lodge's various rooms to look for such a blanket. The lodge agreed, and assigned Cary Stayner to help the agents with the search. As one of the lodge's maintenance men, Cary had a key to all the rooms; additionally, the lodge felt that Cary was one of their steadiest and most reliable employees.

Thus, on May 26, 1999, Cary Stayner accompanied the agents from room to room in the lodge as they searched for a blanket or other similar object with fibers that might match those found with Dykes, Larwick, and the third man. Everyone present later recalled how polite, pleasant, and helpful Cary Stayner was during the search.

By the first of June, investigators had met with Rufus Dykes numerous times, and each time they sat down with him, his story seemed to change. At first, he said that his half-brother had committed the crimes, and that his only role was to help dispose of the stolen property. But after being confronted with the pink fiber evidence,

Rufus amended his statement: he'd actually helped transport the bodies.

But Rufus was like quicksilver: he was all over the place, and you couldn't pin him down. The thing that frustrated investigators the most was that Rufus seemed genuinely unable to tell how, when, where, and why the killings were committed.

That gave the TOURNAP task force doubts; while most believed that Larwick and Dykes had to be somehow involved, they were also aware that they were significantly short of evidence necessary to prove a case to a jury beyond a reasonable doubt.

One example was the ring story: Dykes had said he'd been given a ring by Larwick; one of the women who testified before the grand jury said *she'd* been given a ring by Larwick, which somehow seemed to dovetail with the tale first reported by Mooney in late April, about the young girl who claimed she'd been given a ring by the "two men" she'd shared methamphetamine with, and who had claimed to have killed Juli Sund in the house in Modesto.

Investigators recovered the ring from the witness, and showed it to Carole Carrington, Carole Sund's mother. Carole Carrington told investigators she was 80 percent sure the ring had belonged to Juli Sund; Juli's younger sister, Gina, said she was 90 percent sure the ring had belonged to Juli.

Eighty percent on a test score is a fine grade, and 90 percent is even better. But in a court of law, even 90 percent amounts to reasonable doubt. So far, there just wasn't enough evidence to bring the half-brothers, or anyone else for that matter, to court.

Nevertheless, by the second week in June, James Maddock was feeling particularly confident that his group was well down the right track in solving the kidnappings and murders.

In fact, Maddock said, he was pretty sure everyone involved in the crimes was currently in jail.

"I do feel we have all the main players in jail," Maddock told a reporter for the Sacramento *Bee*, Cynthia Hubert. "But we are in no rush to charge them."

One of the main problems faced by investigators, Maddock said, was that the memories of many of the witnesses so far interviewed were faulty, in part because of habitual drug use; in addition, the investigation was hampered by "the extraordinary lengths" the perpetrators went to in order to conceal evidence.

Not only that, Maddock said, his people were still having a hard time developing a clear motive for the crimes. Was it done for money? Was it a robbery gone bad? A kidnapping for ransom? A sex crime? It was all too fuzzy, Maddock admitted, and even contradictory.

"The problem is that many of the people we are dealing with as potential witnesses are members of a crankster circle," Maddock said, referring to habitual methamphetamine users. "They deal in the meathamphetamine trade and they have a lot of baggage. These are dopers who can't remember what they did yesterday, much less weeks ago, or where a suspect was on a particular day, at a particular time."

Later, Maddock's critics—including his longtime nemesis, Senator Grassley of Iowa—would point to this and similar statements by Maddock as evidence that he had unintentionally gulled the public into concluding that the threat at Yosemite was over: that, indeed, "we have all the main players in jail." And even Maddock was to wish he could take those words back and consign them to oblivion.

But Nick Rossi was later to point out that Maddock's remarks had to be taken in the context of the question: as reporters kept pressing the FBI man as to when the "rogues" were going to be charged, Maddock had simply pointed out that there was no real urgency in laying charges since they were all in jail. But the way Maddock worded his remark, it sounded as if he were saying that the federals had rounded up everyone who needed it, which wasn't what Maddock meant to say at all.

But the pressure on Maddock only increased two days later, when the *Chronicle* reported that Rufus Dykes had confessed to the murders.

TWENTY-THREE

"A KEY SUSPECT IN THE SLAYING OF three Yosemite tourists has admitted involvement in the killings, a law enforcement source close to the case said yesterday," the *Chronicle*'s Stacy Finz reported on June 12.

Rufus Dykes had admitted his involvement in the murders, Finz's unnamed source said.

"We're now trying to confirm his involvement," Finz quoted the "official" as saying. "Confessions are very susceptible to attacks by defense attorneys. We may just have to rely on just his word(s), but we're doing the best we can to corroborate them."

Finz's source wouldn't provide any details about Dykes's supposed admissions; for one thing, investigators themselves still weren't sure what to make of his claims.

Nor would the unnamed sources "officially" link Larwick to the murders, Finz reported.

"We've said from the beginning of this investigation

that we're not going to identify suspects by name until all the facts have been established and charges have been filed," Nick Rossi said.

Still, the gate was open and the monster was out: the reports in the Sacramento *Bee*, the *Chronicle*, the *Examiner*, the Modesto *Bee* and the Associated Press all left the clear impression that James Maddock and his people had zeroed in on Larwick, Dykes et al, and it was only a matter of days or weeks before the "rogues" would be hailed into court on the kidnapping and murders of Carole, Juli, and Silvina.

Realizing that he had probably gone too far in suggesting that *all* the people involved in the crimes were already in custody, Maddock tried to backpedal a bit by observing that the investigation wasn't complete; and several days later, Rossi raised the possibility that more arrests might occur. But it was too late; readers had already been left with the notion that for all practical purposes, the disappearances and murders of the three women had been solved.

Soon information leaked about about the fiber evidence.

"Federal authorities yesterday," the *Chronicle*'s Finz and Pamela Podger reported on Monday, June 14, "said they found fibers and other physical evidence that connect a loose-knit group of ex-convicts living in the central valley to the mysterious abductions and killings of the women."

That seemed to clinch matters: with a reported confession from Dykes and physical evidence, what more did the FBI need?

Well, motive for one thing, along with details on how the crimes unfolded. In this regard, Dykes had been unhelpful, while Larwick continued to maintain that he'd had nothing to do with the crime. Dykes's continued imprecision was attributed either to his faulty, supposedly drug-addled memory, or his desire to negotiate a plea deal with the authorities. So far, the *Chronicle* reported, no such deal had been offered to Dykes.

The Associated Press at this juncture distributed a fairly detailed account of the lives of the two now-notorious half-brothers and their families. Both Dykes and Larwick had spent extensive time in prison, as had Dykes's father, Eugene Burel Dykes; the men had different fathers but the same mother, whose full name was not used in the article.

The last time the mother had seen the two half-brothers at the same time was in 1991, at the visiting compound of a state prison in Ione, California; Michael Larwick was just finishing his term at the prison, while Rufus Dykes was just starting his.

At least three times over the years, the two brothers had been in the same jail at the same time, once at Soledad State Prison.

Gene Burel Dykes was also present at the Ione prison visiting compound at the 1991 visit, AP reporter Christine Hanley recounted. By 1999, Dykes's father was now 67 years old and suffering from heart problems, diabetes, and colon cancer. But in his younger days, Burel Dykes had been something of a hellraiser himself. He served a dozen years in San Quentin for "everything short of murder," as he put it to Hanley. His own father, Burel added, had been shot dead in a street robbery when Burel was just a boy. Burel had wound up in reform school, where he'd lost three fingers to a meat grinder. But after his extended stay in San Quentin, Burel went straight.

"It's been 40 years since I got out," he said. "I never got in trouble again, and they still ain't forgotten. Anything bad happens, it's my fault. There's so many things people don't see."

Neither Burel or the half-brothers' mother believed that Michael or Rufus had anything to do with the murders of Carole, Silvina, and Juli, Hanley reported.

But they admitted that life hadn't been easy for either of the sons. Larwick was a small boy when his mother and her two other children took up with Burel, after leaving Leroy Larwick; soon little Gene, who would later come to be called Rufus, was born, an event that Burel claimed caused the boys' mother to try to kill herself. Eventually Larwick's mother took Michael and the other two children and left Burel, leaving little Gene in his father's custody.

"It got ugly," Larwick's mother recounted to Hanley. "I gave Gene [Rufus] up for my freedom, for myself, and my three children to be on our own. There was no other way to do it." Little Gene was just three years old at the time.

And there it was, the answer to the question posed at the Modesto vigil by Joe Klass, who wondered why we live in a country where a mother and two young girls can't even visit a national park without running the risk of violent death at the hands of predatory criminals. The story of Dykes and Larwick is the story of crime in America: poverty, family violence, self-hatred, revenge, desperation, institutions that warehouse the disturbed and abandoned until the space is needed for the still-more violent. These were exactly the sorts of things that someone like Carole Sund understood all too well; and it was the ultimate bitter irony that they were the very forces that in the end directly caused her disappearance and grisly death.

Even though neither Michael Larwick nor Rufus Dykes had anything to do with it.

EL PORTAL
JUNE 21, 1999

TWENTY-FOUR

By the middle of June, 1999, the FBI's Maddock and Rossi had finally quit talking, reasoning that the more they said, the more the media demanded.

"It was a strange relationship," one of the FBI men recalled afterward. In the beginning, the Bureau wanted the help of the public in looking for the missing tourists and their car, and for that help, it was decided to give the news media as much cooperation as possible.

And, in the beginning, at least, it worked. "The publicity helped that car to be discovered," one agent said. If it hadn't been for the constant news reports—buttressed as they were by the Sund-Carrington reward offers—it was quite likely that the burned-out vehicle would have been overlooked by the average passerby. The fire had so completely consumed the car that it appeared to have been there a very long time, the FBI was to say later. It was only the publicity about the missing car that gave its discoverer the incentive for a closer look.

But in making themselves so available to the news media, the FBI had created an insatiable monster: once on the story, the news outlets pressed for more, more, and still more. Once the Bureau and the local authorities began to look at possible perpetrators, the media wanted the details on that, as well.

"From very early in the case," one agent recalled, "the press was eager to report on suspects." And while Maddock, Rossi, and others held steadfastly to their commitment not to discuss individual suspects, their actions could not be kept secret—not when friends and relatives of those questioned readily admitted that the FBI had been paying visits, tearing up carpet swatches, and generally poking through the "rogues'" backgrounds.

It began with Billy Joe Strange, and soon escalated to Larwick and Dykes. With the latter two, the media at least had something solid to chew on—Larwick's long criminal history practically assured him the spotlight; and after the "just wondering" column by Diane Nelson in the Modesto *Bee*, hardly a day went by when the FBI wasn't peppered with questions as to when it was going to charge Larwick with the murders and get it over with. And once it was widely reported that Dykes had confessed to the crimes, and Maddock had told the Sacramento *Bee*'s Cynthia Hubert that the TOURNAP task force believed it had all the players behind bars, the FBI realized that it was time to clam up, really and truly.

Thus, more than a month passed in the FBI's newly vowed silence, and the news reports about the Yosemite murders dwindled away; based on the reports of early June, many assumed that all the bad guys were locked up, and it would only be a matter of time before charges were brought.

It was Wednesday, July 21, 1999, in the late afternoon when 26-year-old Joie Ruth Armstrong, a petite strawberry-blond naturalist who worked for a nonprofit educational foundation at Yosemite National Park, began packing for a weekend trip to visit a friend north of San Francisco. The car was just about ready, and she'd just answered a call from a nearby neighbor, a coworker at the Yosemite Institute. The coworker wanted some paperwork, and Joie said she'd bring it right over before leaving on her trip.

But the killer had other ideas. He'd been watching Joie for some time as she'd loaded the car. Now he drove his truck down the dirt track toward the house Joie shared with two others, stopped, and got out to talk. The front door to Joie's house stood open, and from inside the killer could hear music from a stereo.

The next sequence of events was confusing. It seems that the killer tried to strike up a conversation with Joie, but wasn't successful. Joie was busy, getting ready to leave, and besides, she had to drop off the paperwork for her coworker, who lived about a five-minute walk away. It was about that time that the killer realized that Joie was alone.

It appears that the killer either followed Joie into the

small house or chased her there. The killer tried to get Joie to cooperate, but that wasn't going to happen. He wanted to tie her up with duct tape, but Joie wasn't going to go for *that*. A fight ensued, the slightly built, 120-pound Joie giving the towering, 200-pound killer some very stiff resistance. The killer produced a large knife, and in the fight Joie sustained some cuts on her arms, which would later clearly be seen as defensive wounds. What happened next would only be learned later by the FBI, and they wouldn't be talking.

All through the night of June 21, Joie's friend in Marin County waited for her to arrive, but she didn't show up. About 3:00 A.M., the friend became worried enough to call the California Highway Patrol, fearing that Joie had become involved in an accident during her drive north. The CHP had no record of any accident involving Joie, but after learning that Joie lived in Yosemite Park, decided to call the park's rangers to let them know about the situation.

Shortly after daybreak on Thursday, July 22, a team of rangers went to Joie's cabin in the Foresta section of the park; to get there, the rangers had to drive up Highway 120 to a turnoff a few miles before Crane Flat, and then descend into the Big Meadow area by way of a long, winding, single-lane asphalt road.

The Foresta area was one of the few residential areas in the park, with clusters of private and publicly owned houses here and there; the house shared by Joie was one of those closest to Big Meadow, and in fact could be seen from the rim of the valley high above, if one were looking for it.

Part of the area had been burned over in an earlier forest fire. Crane Flat Creek, which began at the rim of the valley so high above, wandered through the Big Meadow and skirted a bank of low hills to the west before entering a tiny rock-strewn canyon that eventually spilled into the Merced River near the El Portal Post Office. A dirt road linked El Portal to Foresta but was closed off by a chain. Thus, the only way into Foresta required a visitor to take Highway 120 to the turnoff just before Crane Flat; and because much of the area was sparsely wooded from the old forest fire, just about any vehicle entering the area was visible for miles as it made its way down the single-lane road.

Just after 7:30 A.M., the park rangers arrived at Joie's cabin. It was apparent that some sort of struggle had taken place inside; the rangers found a pair of broken sunglasses that had been bent and crushed on the living room floor. One of Joie's roommates later said he'd never seen the sunglasses before. It therefore appeared that an intruder had come into the house and that a violent struggle had ensued. A search for Joie and any additional evidence was begun.

Other rangers searched the nearby homes, and at one house, learned that Joie had promised by telephone to bring the paperwork over to the neighbor within a few minutes. That call had happened at about 6:30 P.M.; at 7:30, the neighbor, concerned about Joie's failure to arrive, had walked over to Joie's cabin and had found her car packed, the front door open, and the stereo playing. But there was no sign of Joie.

The rangers began a traditional search pattern, working outward from the cabin. About 1:30 that afternoon, the body of Joie Armstrong was found floating in Crane Creek less than 100 yards from the cabin. The head was missing, apparently severed from the body by a large, heavy knife.

Within a matter of hours, Mariposa County Sheriff's deputies and representatives of the FBI were on the scene. Because the murder of Joie Armstrong had taken place on U.S. Government property, this time the jurisdiction clearly belonged to the Bureau. Special efforts were taken to preserve the crime scene, and Joie's body was left where it was found in the water for the time being. A cursory search for the head was undertaken, but it couldn't be located.

A new search of the area now began. This time an employee of the park's fire department recalled seeing an older model white-on-blue International Scout four-wheel-drive vehicle the previous night in the area of Joie's cabin at about 7:30 P.M.—almost the same time that the neighbor was on her way over to check on Joie.

Another park employee recalled picking up a man in the park between 10:00 and 10:30 P.M. the night before, on July 21. The man had been standing off to the side of Highway 140, next to a white-on-blue International Scout truck, which he claimed had broken down. The man explained to the park employee that he'd been inside the park to get some "decent food."

The employee gave the man a ride to Cedar Lodge, where he said he lived.

Based on the two accounts, an alert was broadcast to rangers and other law enforcement officers to be on the lookout for a white-on-blue International Scout truck. At about 4:30 P.M. on July 22, even as rangers, deputy sheriffs, and FBI agents were still processing the crime scene at Foresta, two park rangers, Bonnie Schwartz and Ruth Middlecamp, were sent to investigate a report of a white-on-blue Scout just outside of the park. Contact was made with the Mariposa Sheriff's Department, which would have jurisdiction outside the park boundaries.

Schwartz was soon joined by Mariposa County detective Cathi Sarno. The pair located the truck, determined that it was registered to Cary Anthony Stayner, and soon encountered Cary sitting nude on a small beach off the Merced River not far from Cedar Lodge. A quick search by the ranger and detective showed that Cary had marijuana in his possession. He also had a dark green backpack.

By this point on the afternoon of July 22, Joie Armstrong's head had still not been found. Schwartz and Sarno eyed Cary's backpack and wondered: if they looked inside, would they see something they would never forget? They asked Cary for permission to look inside the backpack, but Cary refused.

The officers escorted Cary back to his truck, and Cary gave permission for the truck to be searched. He still refused to let the officers look inside the backpack, even when they told him that if they found more drugs they would only seize them, not charge him with any drug violations.

Cary still refused to let them look inside the back-pack; at that point, the officers told Cary that the back-pack would be seized whether Cary liked it or not, and that a warrant would be obtained to make a legal search of its contents. By this point the officers had begun to wonder what Cary was so anxious to hide. Was it, they wondered, the severed head of Joie Armstrong?

But once Cary learned that the officers intended to take possession of the backpack, he relented: Go ahead and search it, he said. But the officers now declined Cary's offer, having become concerned that if the head were found inside, a later legal issue might arise as to the voluntariness of Stayner's consent to search.

Instead, Stayner and the backpack were taken to the rangers' nearby headquarters in El Portal for further questioning, while an additional examination of the Scout was conducted.

In an interview begun about 9:00 P.M. on July 22 by Rangers Schwartz, Jeff Sullivan, and FBI Agent Jeff Kearl, Cary denied being in the Foresta area at any time on the previous day. He'd been in Yosemite Valley all day, he said, and hadn't gone up Highway 120.

What had he been up to while in the valley? Cary was asked. He'd been swimming, Cary told Schwartz. Afterward, he'd gone back to El Portal to change his clothes. Following this, he'd driven back into the park for dinner.

This seemed weird to Schwartz, because the drive into and out of the park on Highway 140 was so difficult and time-consuming, what with road construction work still underway. Why would someone make *four* trips up and down Highway 140 on such a terrible road, which ran for more than seven miles from El Portal to the end of the construction zone—in all, 28 miles of arduous driving? And hadn't Stayner told the park employee the night before that his truck had broken down? If it was in such bad mechanical shape, why drive the bad road four times in one day?

While Stayner was being interviewed, another ranger and a professional tracker, Mark Fincher, was comparing photographs he had taken of tire tracks found near Joie's cabin—and near the place in the creek where her body was found—with similar photographs taken by Sullivan and Kearl of the tires on Cary's truck.

In Fincher's opinion, the tracks found at the cabin were similar to those of the Scout's tires.

Despite the fireman's account, and Fincher's belief that the tires on Cary's truck were similar to those found at Joie's cabin, it was clear that authorities didn't have enough information to arrest Cary. Late on the night of July 22, Cary was released, along with his Scout. The backpack, still unopened, was kept, however.

Cary's movements over the next 24 hours were not immediately clear. It appeared that Stayner drove to Cedar Lodge, where he still had his room over the restaurant. It appeared that he sold his television set and VCR to a coworker for $150 in cash and a promise to pay $125 later. Afterward, Cary went into the lounge, where he encountered a friend, and complained that the rangers had searched his truck and seized his backpack. He seemed angry, the friend recalled later.

Agents later learned that around 1:00 A.M. on July 23, three hours after the end of his interrogation at the ranger station, and after selling his television set and VCR, Cary had gone to visit a woman friend in El Portal. Usually, Cary rarely came calling so late and unnounced. Cary stayed about five minutes, and complained that there was something wrong with the Scout, and that he might need a tow truck. After about five minutes, Cary left. The Scout seemed to start right up, the woman friend noticed.

And with that, Cary disappeared into the night.

TWENTY-FIVE

THE FOLLOWING DAY, JULY 23, authorities decided to talk to Cary some more; but when they went to Cedar Lodge to pick him up, they found that he'd never reported to work that day. The lodge manager said that was very unusual for Cary; in fact it had only happened once before in the two years Cary had worked at the lodge. Another all-points bulletin was issued for Cary's Scout, and this time, Cary himself.

About 2:30 that afternoon, Joie's headless body was removed from the creek, and a more thorough search of the creekbed was made. About 5:30 P.M., the head was located underwater and about 40 yards downstream.

That same afternoon, a warrant was obtained to search the suspicious backpack. A park ranger opened it and discovered a melange of articles, none of which jumped out as suggestive of evidence of murder: two towels, a beer bottle, tanning lotion, a harmonica, breath mints, an X-Acto knife, several scraps of paper, a used Band-Aid, and a collection of coins. The two most interesting items were a Polaroid camera, and a copy of a novel, *Black Lightning*—which turned about to be about a serial killer.

Why was Cary so paranoid about the backpack? No one at the time offered any explanantion for his behavior, at least publicly. There weren't any additional drugs in the backpack, and certainly the X-Acto knife hadn't been used to cut Joie Armstrong's head off, so why was Cary Stayner so nervous about its search?

One possibility—and the FBI never addressed this with any of the news media at the time—was that the camera itself might have been the cause of Stayner's anxiety. But since Polaroid cameras by their nature don't have exposed film in them, the only remaining possibility was that Stayner knew the camera did not belong to him, and that it would not be long before the authorities realized that, and traced it to its original owner—possibly Carole, Juli, or Silvina.

In any event, by the night of Friday, July 23, Cary Stayner was long gone, and the search was on.

The news of another murder associated with Yosemite put James Maddock right where he no longer wanted to be—in the media's red glare. And this time, there would be no quarter.

In a press briefing Friday afternoon, Maddock said agents were working on a number of leads. He could have, at that point, told the press that an all-points bulletin had been issued for Cary Stayner and his Scout, but didn't. Maddock was still following the rules of not mentioning suspects' names until they were charged.

"We do have a number of leads," Maddock said, "some of which show promise. But that doesn't mean we have a suspect identified."

Maddock was so gunshy of the media at this point that he refused to even confirm Joie's identity; that he wouldn't comment on her manner of death was to be expected.

Naturally, the question everyone wanted to know was whether the latest death was connected to the Sund-Pelosso case.

Maddock said there was no apparent connection. But the papers quickly noted that the Bureau had sent agents to Cedar Lodge, and said workers at the lodge were claiming that agents had questioned a maintenance worker and had searched his vehicle.

From that, it didn't take the reporters long to find out that the worker who was questioned was Cary Stayner—none other than the older brother of Steven Stayner, so famous so many years before. Workers at the lodge told them that FBI agents had gone door-to-door in the worker living quarters, showing a pair of smashed sunglasses, and asking whether they belonged to Stayner. Later, the Mariposa County authorities confirmed that an all-points bulletin had been issued for Cary Stayner and his truck.

The *Chronicle*'s Stacy Finz and two other reporters, in an apparent scoop over their *Examiner* rivals, reported that a "sweeping manhunt" was underway for Cary.

"While FBI officials refused to comment about the status of the Armstrong case, sources close to the investigation confirmed that Stayner is the focus of the probe and that search warrants will be drawn up today." Actually the warrants had already been drawn, signed, and served by Friday evening.

Finz and her colleagues rapidly contacted Del and Kay Stayner, who by now were living in Atwater, just outside Merced. Del said he had no idea where Cary had gone; in fact, he planned to report him as a missing person.

Based on the reporters' questions, Del soon realized that some people believed that Cary was responsible for Joie's murder. That just didn't compute, as far as Del was concerned.

"What I'm worried about," Del said, "is that he might have seen something he wasn't supposed to. We lived through this before and it's not very funny. My little boy Stevie went missing for seven and a half years. That's my middle son, and now my oldest son is missing." The situation was tearing him up, Del added.

Cary had never mentioned knowing Joie, Del added. He confirmed that although Wednesday and Thursday were Cary's normal days off at the lodge, he had still been up at Yosemite.

At that point in their piece, the *Chronicle* returned to Maddock's press conference.

"We have no reason to believe there is a continuing threat," Maddock said, in reference to people visiting or working at Yosemite. "I have reason to believe a killer is loose somewhere, but I don't believe the killer is planning another crime."

The news about the "sweeping manhunt" couldn't be kept quiet, no matter how much the FBI refused to talk about suspects. By the time *Chronicle* readers were learning about the search for Stayner over their Saturday morning coffee, Stayner was already being taken into custody. The reason: publicity about the "manhunt" had been broadcast on a news report aired Saturday morning.

As it happened, Stayner had left El Portal early on the morning of July 23, and had driven down to a nudist resort in Wilton, California, about 25 miles southeast of Sacramento on the Cosumnes River.

Stayner checked into the Laguna del Sol resort that afternoon. That evening he introduced himself to a woman resident. The next morning, the woman heard the broadcast about the manhunt, and immediately called the FBI.

By 9:00 A.M. on Saturday, July 24, as Cary was eating breakfast at the resort's restaurant, about a half-dozen FBI agents and Sacramento County Sheriff's deputies came in and surrounded him. Cary immediately stood up and raised his hands. The agents cuffed him and walked him out the door on the way to the Sacramento County Jail.

This is probably a good place to consider a few interesting aspects of the events of Thursday, Friday, and Saturday following Joie Armstrong's murder.

Why, for example, had Stayner told two different people that there was something wrong with his truck? Indeed, why had he left it in the park on the night of July 21, when he hitched a ride back to Cedar Lodge with the park employee? It seemed clear later that there was nothing at all wrong with the Scout.

The fact that Stayner told two different people that there were mechnical problems with the truck, however, suggests the possibility that he was preparing an alibi for Wednesday night—the night Joie was killed. If he left his truck along Highway 140 inside the park that night, it was always possible that someone else had used it to do the deed—or at least, Cary might be able to claim that later. He had two witnesses to back him up—a park employee who had picked him up, and the woman friend he'd seen shortly after his first lengthy interrogation.

A second point about the events: by the afternoon of Friday, July 23, Maddock and the other FBI men were so reticent about being connected to the names of any suspects that their refusal to announce that Cary Stayner and his truck were being sought actually might have made it far harder to apprehend Stayner the following day. Had the news reporters simply accepted Maddock's no-names edict without checking at Cedar Lodge—and if the Mariposa County Sheriff's Department hadn't confirmed that he was being sought—the woman at the nudist resort would never have known to call the FBI to report Stayner's whereabouts the following day. Once again, publicity was proven a useful tool for law enforcement, provided it was handled correctly.

And one final point: certainly Cary Stayner by Friday afternoon had realized that he would be the focus of the FBI's investigation of the murder of Joie Armstrong—that much Stayner himself made clear later, as we shall see. So why did Stayner introduce himself to the woman at the nudist camp Friday night with his own, real name?

Here is a possible insight into the personality of Cary Stayner: for all his life he had lived in the reflected light cast by the amazing story of his younger brother Steven's return from the missing after seven years; indeed, it appears that while Michael Larwick's claim to fame as a lad was that he was the son of the man who said he'd gotten Bigfoot on film, Cary Stayner's own claim to be somebody was to be the brother of the little boy who'd been kidnapped and who had returned to tell about it; in fact, it appears that using this story was Cary Stayner's favorite pick-up line.

TWENTY-SIX

STAYNER'S ARREST WAS ANnounced Saturday by Maddock at another press conference Saturday afternoon. Maddock said he would have a "significant announcement" the next day at another news conference that would be held in Sacramento.

"Within the past twenty-four hours," Maddock said, "we have made tremendous progress on the investigation of [the] Joie Armstrong [case]," Maddock told reporters.

And then Maddock had to swallow the bitter medicine that had been awaiting him ever since his remark in June about "all the players" in the Sund-Pelosso murders being in jail. "I have information within the last twenty-four hours," Maddock said, "that may cause me to modify my statement."

What Maddock had, however, was a confession from Cary Stayner, claiming responsibility not only for the Joie Armstrong murder, but the kidnappings and murders of Carole, Juli, and Silvina as well.

* * *

The way it was reconstructed later by the ubiquitous "sources familiar with the investigation," Cary Stayner began confessing to all of the crimes almost as soon as he could once he was taken into custody. Advised of his rights to remain silent and to consult with a lawyer, Stayner waived them; it was almost as if he were eager to tell the authorities what he had done. A video camera was set up, and Stayner began his grim recital.

Stayner readily admitted killing Joie Armstrong and decapitating her. Then, in the same, calm, almost detached voice, he acknowledged kidnapping and killing Carole, Juli, and Silvina five months earlier. Stayner's description of his crimes against all of the victims were so precise and conformed so well to the evidence that the authorities had that the FBI's most experienced interrogators were convinced Stayner was telling the truth. Based on Stayner's statements, agents fanned out to various locations, and soon were returning with corroborating evidence, including at least one knife capable of severing a head, and the long-sought pink blanket that had been used to cover Juli Sund—the very one Stayner himself had once helped agents search for. All through Saturday Stayner talked, until by the end of the day, the FBI's experts were just beginning to realize: they had captured a man whose very innocuousness had masked one of the most lethal predators since the days of Ted Bundy.

The following day, Sunday, July 25, Special Agent in Charge James Maddock stood in front of a brace of microphones at the United States Courthouse in Sacramento, and had to admit it:

"We have developed specific information linking Stayner to the Sund-Pelosso murders," he said. And then he added: "We believe we have the responsible party for all of these murders."

After all the months chasing down the rogues, after all the forensic tests on fibers, after all the polygraph examinations, grand jury testimony, wild tales from wild women about rings and drugs and check forgeries, this is what it actually came down to: a seemingly mild-mannered maintenance man who had been under the FBI's collective noses from the very beginning had freely *admitted* to the crimes.

Maddock looked haggard; he knew that his butt was firmly in the sling—especially since his inadvertant statement in June that claimed "all the players" in the Sund-Pelosso case were locked up on other charges. It would not be long—a day, maybe sooner than that—before someone would ask the dreaded question: if the FBI had been just a bit quicker on the uptake, just a bit more proficient . . . would Joie Armstrong still be alive?

It was probably the worst moment of Maddock's public life, but he forged ahead.

"I have asked myself," Maddock said, "whether we could have done anything differently that might have prevented the murder of Joie Armstrong. I have struggled with that issue for the last twenty-four hours and continue to do so . . ."

Maddock paused for a minute, and then looked back

at the assembled news people staring at him with all
the fascination of a crowd watching a car wreck in slow
motion.

"I'm confident we've done everything that could
have been done," he said.

His mea culpa aside, Maddock still wasn't ready to
concede that the TOURNAP task force had been headed
off on a wild rogue chase all along.

"We are looking at whether [Stayner] is solely responsible, or if others are involved." But Maddock admitted: so far, no one had come up with any evidence
that Stayner knew any of those who had long been
mentioned as suspects in the case, such as Larwick and
Dykes.

Even as Maddock was serving himself up on the
media's sacrificial altar, Stayner himself was leading
the FBI on a tour of various locations associated with
the crimes. Agents used a video-camera and docu-
mented Stayner re-enacting the murder of Joie Armstrong; later, Stayner accompanied agents on a tour of
the Sund-Pelosso sites, pointing out the precise locations, and explaining what he had done and how he had
done it. With his earlier videotaped confession, and the
evidence Stayner had told agents where to find, the case
against Cary Stayner for the murder of Joie Armstrong
looked virtually unassailable. That is, it looked that
way if Stayner wasn't fronting for someone else, claiming for himself all the details of the crimes that someone else had committed. It that was the case, it would
be for reasons that no one could readily fathom.

*   *   *

The naming of Stayner as the party responsible for the murders that had mesmerized the nation for much of the previous five months in turn launched the newspeople in some new directions: just who *was* Cary Stayner, and why would he do such things? Most of all, why would he so readily confess?

Reporters soon tracked Stayner's history back to El Portal, and eventually Merced. Almost invariably, people who had known Stayner for years were flabbergasted, not the least his own family.

Del Stayner, cornered in the mobile home he shared with Kay, refused to come outside to be photographed. Asked through a screen door by a television reporter whether he believed that Cary had committed the crimes, an obviously brokenhearted Del said he couldn't believe it; it just wasn't in his son's nature to be violent.

Del gave similar comments to the newspapers.

"He's the nicest guy you'd ever want to meet," he told the *Chronicle*.

A former Stayner neighbor in Merced, Linda Shertz, told the *Examiner* that she simply couldn't imagine that Cary Stayner could have done such things. "I can't imagine that he would be capable of abducting three people and keeping them—especially after what happened to his brother."

The ghost of Steven Stayner was resurrected by the news outlets, who briefly recapped his kidnapping and return from the lost so many years earlier. The *Chronicle* tracked down former Merced detective Bill Bailey, now retired, who was the first to float a possible explanation of Cary's self-confessed behavior.

"I'd say the whole Stayner family was pretty well-traumatized by the Steven kidnapping," Bailey said, hinting at the underlying issues that had affected the Stayner family for so long.

Other reporters went to El Portal, where they tried to develop a portrait of Cary Stayner. Reporters interviewed Jesse Houtz, the proprietor of Cedar Lodge, who had rented Room Number 4 above his establishment to Cary for more than two years.

"He was a nice guy," Houtz said. "He kept pretty much to himself. He was very pleasant." Houtz said Cary would occasionally hang out at the restaurant's lounge, but that he wasn't a particularly heavy drinker. "He knew everyone and talked to everyone," Houtz said, "but I can't say whether anyone was his best friend or not."

One of Cary's coworkers at the lodge, Al Sanchez, recalled Cary as a nice guy who liked to joke around with others, even if he was quiet pretty much of the time. "I don't think he did it," said Sanchez. "He just seemed like a regular person."

Another El Portal resident, Nancy Wilson, painted a slightly darker picture of Cary: Stayner, she said, was fond of nude sunbathing along the river, and that he sometimes approached teenaged girls along the river, explaining his nudity by claiming to be a sun worshipper. It seemed to Wilson that Stayner usually steered clear of older women, favoring teenagers instead.

Others told how Cary enjoyed smoking marijuana and hiking in the park; if he had one passion, some said, it was an abiding belief in Bigfoot . . .

Over the next several weeks, even as Stayner was making his way through the federal legal system, still other stories about Stayner began to come forth; indeed, old Stayner stories began to proliferate as many people in El Portal and Merced struggled to describe the man they thought they knew.

A San Francisco radio reporter told several national television shows that early in the search for Carole, Juli, and Silvina, she had found herself alone in a hot tub with Cary at Cedar Lodge. The reporter said she'd asked Cary what he thought had happened to the missing tourists, and Cary, like most other employees of the lodge, said he didn't have the slightest idea. Then, said the reporter, Cary had introduced himself, using his full name. That led into Cary's story about the kidnapping of his younger brother so many years before. The radio reporter recalled the story, and as she watched and listened to Cary recount it, she said later, she began to pick up weird vibes from Cary. Suddenly realizing she was alone with a man she barely knew, at some distance from anyone else, she quickly got out of the hot tub and went to her room and deadbolted the door. The next day, she said, she'd called someone in law enforcement to suggest that they take a hard look at Cary Stayner, but was told that Cary had been cleared as a suspect.

Neighbors of the Stayners and old high school acquaintances recalled Cary as introverted, whose main passion was drawing cartoons. Many believed that if they ever heard of Cary again in the future, it would be as a professional cartoonist.

But others recalled more of Cary's dark side. One woman, who grew up in the Stayner family neighborhood, recalled Cary exposing himself to her and one of Cary's sisters. She thought Cary was "perverted" at the time, but never dreamed he would wind up accused of a serial killing spree.

Many of those interviewed in Merced laid Cary's problems to the kidnapping of Steven. Linda Shertz, for one, thought that Cary had been traumatized by the kidnapping, and even more traumatized by Steven's unexpected return. After Steven came back, the whole family's focus was on Steven, Shertz recalled, and Cary was relegated to the background.

"Everything they did," Shertz said of the Stayners, "everything they had, it was about Steven."

The *Examiner*'s Michael Dougan and Elizabeth Fernandez attempted to delve into Cary's upbringing in search of motivations for murder.

They tracked down a San Jose State University sociologist, P. Terry McDonald, who specialized in the psychology of multiple murderers. McDonald said that multiple killers often begin their fantasies and eventual criminal activities after the failure of an important relationship.

"I suspect," McDonald told Dougan and Fernandez, "he has had some failed relationships that turned out pretty bad."

Another expert, San Francisco State criminologist Mike Rustigan, told Dougan and Fernandez that sometimes serial killers have "abandonment" issues as children.

"Sometimes you find a lack of any bonding between child and parents."

The two reporters next tracked down author Mike Echols, who wrote a book about Steven Stayner's kidnapping that later formed the basis of the television movie, "I Know My Name Is Steven."

In Echols's view, the disappearance of Steven Stayner, followed by his reappearance so many years later, effectively rendered Cary Stayner, the oldest son, into almost a non-person.

Echols had spent considerable time with the Stayners while he was writing his book, and he believed that while Kay Stayner felt very responsible for the children's physical well-being, she simply wasn't very comfortable in expressing affection.

Once, Echols said, he had joined the Stayner family for dinner after Steven had returned.

"After Kay walked back to the stove after setting the table," Echols recalled for Dougan and Fernandez, "Steven remarked to her that she had forgotten one place setting. 'Who?' she said, and Steven pointed over to his brother. 'Oh yes,' she said, 'Cary.' "

Another strain on the Stayner family was Steven's former walk-on-the-wild-side habits he'd picked up while under Parnell's influence.

Back in the early '80s, both brothers experimented with drugs, Echols said.

"The thing is, Cary got in trouble for it, and Steven didn't . . . A lot of slack was cut for Steven . . . he could do no wrong, and Cary became something of a scape-goat. He was the whipping boy for the fair-haired prince."

That Cary seemed pushed into the background of his own family seemed to be confirmed by Del Stayner's own sister, Anita Jones, who told the Sacramento *Bee* that Steven got all the attention.

"Whatever Steven wanted," the *Bee* quoted her, "Steven got."

TWENTY-SEVEN

THE DAY AFTER THE COURTHOUSE press conference, after he had led agents on the guided tour of the sites of his depredations, Stayner was scheduled to make his initial appearance in court in Sacramento. While not much was expected to happen, it would represent the chance to see the man everyone had been talking about in person for the first name, and as a result, every news media outfit in northern California was on hand.

Among those in attendance was a 32-year-old television reporter for a San Jose station that had a sister outlet in San Francisco, Ted Rowlands, of stations KNTV and KBWB.

Ted had been in the television news business for about eight years. A graduate of the University of Wisconsin, he'd begun his career as a sports reporter in Duluth, Minnesota. He'd spent almost four years there before getting another (and warmer) job in Salinas, California. Since then, he'd been slowly working his way up the coast.

By the time of the Sund-Pelosso disappearances, Ted had been off the sports beat for some time. He'd covered the Sund-Pelosso case from the beginning; now he was in Sacramento with his cameraman, Walt Colby, preparing for Stayner's initial court appearance.

As far as Rowlands could see, this would be a fairly routine assignment, even if it was expected to be well watched in the Bay Area; after all, the Sund-Pelosso case had been saturating the news for months.

Rowlands had followed all the ups and downs with the rogues; while he admitted he was no expert, there was something about the notion that the rogues were responsible for the Sund-Pelosso murders that had been bothering Rowlands for some time.

For one thing, people like Larwick and Dykes simply seemed too disorganized to have pulled off the kidnapping and its apparent coverup. These were people, Rowlands realized, who were *impulsive* criminals, not clever, strategic planners. And their crimes had been committed for immediate gain: where was their motive in kidnapping and then murdering Carole, Juli, and Silvina? People like Larwick and Dykes might rob them, sure, or even rape them, maybe (even though the rogues' previous sex crimes had all involved people they knew, not complete strangers). But to kidnap the trio, to murder one and dump her body more than 50 miles away, and then to take the car with two more bodies in it still another 50 or 60 miles away and then

burn it? It all seemed beyond their capabilities to Rowlands. Much the same might be said about the others
whose names had been mentioned, like Billy Joe
Strange.

And the fact that the federal grand jury had been at
work for three months in Fresno with still no apparent
results increased Rowlands's doubts. People like the
rogues would have cracked long before this, he'd figured.

Besides all this, there was the anonymous tip that
had led to the discovery of Juli's body.

"We'd heard they'd been tipped," Rowlands said
later. And if the FBI had been tipped even as they were
looking at Larwick, Dykes, and the others, didn't that
suggest that the information had come from someone
else?

In any event, Rowlands was at home on Saturday,
July 24, when he'd received a page from his office
informing him that someone named Cary Stayner had
been arrested in conncection with the Joie Armstrong
murder. Rowlands and Colby packed up and rushed off
to Maddock's first press conference on Saturday, and
then adjourned to Sacramento Sunday for Maddock's
admission that Stayner was probably responsible for all
the crimes. By then, Rowlands said later, he'd already
guessed that Stayner had to be responsible for all the
murders, simply because the Armstrong killing was so
bizarre, much like the Sund-Pelosso case.

On Monday, as Stayner was preparing for his first
court appearance, Rowlands and Colby made their own
preparations. They decided to get a mug shot of Stayner

from the Sacramento jail, since they knew cameras aren't allowed in federal courtrooms. At just after 7:00 A.M., Rowlands went to the jail and got the mug shot. On the off chance, he asked the jailer whether Stayner would agree to an interview. The jailer laughed; it hardly seemed likely, but the jailer offered to call up to the tier housing Stayner. The answer came back: no way.

Rowlands figured as much. He and Colby went out to breakfast, and considered going back to bed for a few hours of sleep before having to make his 11:00 A.M. news report, but decided against it; Colby wanted to reshoot something, so the pair kept working.

Rowlands returned to the jail and figured it wouldn't hurt to make another request for an interview with Stayner; this time the word came back that Rowlands should check back later.

After Stayner made his 1:30 P.M. appearance, Rowlands and Colby rushed downstairs to get the public defender assigned to Stayner on tape, and he and Colby began work on their later broadcast pieces.

The day was extremely hot, and as Colby manipulated the tape system to prepare the pieces, Rowlands decided to go back to the jail, where at least he could sit down where it was air-conditioned.

Throughout the afternoon, Rowlands shuttled back and forth between the jail and Colby; sometime during the afternoon he made a third request for an interview, which Stayner denied again.

Rowlands did his 5:00 P.M. report, and went back to the jail. The same jailer who'd been there at 7:00 A.M. was still on duty.

"Well, I decided to check one more time," Rowlands recalled. The jailer laughed once more, but called upstairs. After a short conversation, the jailer hung up the telephone and turned to Rowlands.

"I'll be damned," she said, "he's going to talk."

Rowlands was nearly flummoxed by this; he had no notepad with him, because he had thought the whole idea was futile from the beginning. The jailer tore off some pieces of scratch paper, which Rowlands tore them into four pieces each. He had a pen from his hotel in his pocket.

Rowlands took the elevator to the appropriate tier, and waited for four minutes for Stayner to come out. They were separated by a glass wall. Each had a telephone to communicate with the other. Altogether, Rowland's interview of Stayner lasted 24 minutes, with Rowlands furiously scribbling notes on his pieces of scratch paper.

"He was very businesslike," Rowlands said later, "almost clinical. He had a very precise and slow demeanor." Every so often, Stayner would stare back at Rowlands and raise his eyebrow, as if to make certain Rowlands got an important point.

But first Stayner wanted to make sure that Rowlands knew there was a condition to the interview.

"What's that?" Rowlands asked.

He was only doing the interview, Stayner said, because he wanted a made-for-television movie to be made about his life. Rowlands had to promise to make contact with movie producers who would do a movie-of-the-week on Stayner.

"He wanted the same thing that his brother had gotten," Rowlands said later.

There it was: a made-for-television movie. Was this the motive for four horrific murders? Rowlands hardly knew what to say. He nodded noncommittally, and Stayner commenced his story.

"I am guilty," he told Rowlands. "I did murder Carole Sund, Juli Sund, Silvina Pelosso, and Joie Armstrong."

He had acted alone, Stayner told Rowlands. No one else was involved.

Stayner went on to explain that he had been thinking of killing female guests at the lodge for months; in fact, he said, he had harbored a rage against women since the age of seven. He often fantasized about getting control over women, he said, and doing what he wanted to them. But he denied that any of the victims were sexually assaulted.

His attack on Carole, Juli, and Silvina began the night of February 15, Stayner said, when he knocked on the door of Room 509 and told the occupants that he was there to fix a leak. Once he gained admittance, he used a gun to freeze all three women. He then tied them up with duct tape, put Silvina and Juli in the bathroom, and shut the door.

Following this, Stayner said, he strangled Carole Sund, and then dragged her body to the front door of the motel room, and put it in the trunk of the Grand Prix. He returned to the motel room, took Silvina out of the bathroom, killed her, and put her body in the trunk as well.

He returned to the motel room a third time, and took Juli from the bathroom. Later that night, he said, he took Juli to the Grand Prix, put her in the car, and drove out of El Portal down Highway 140 to Highway 49, then up to the scenic overlook near Lake Don Pedro. After removing Juli from the car and carrying her to the ravine, he killed her by cutting her throat with a heavy knife about an hour before dawn.

Returning to the car, Stayner said, he then drove north on Highway 49 to Highway 108, and began climbing into the mountains. Just about a mile or so before Long Barn, he turned off the highway onto a logging road, and then took a second fork. The car got jammed on a hump in the road, and Stayner couldn't drive it any farther.

Stayner said he got out of the car and walked back to the highway, then down the road to Sierra Village. Later that morning he called a taxi in Sonora, about 20 miles away; the cab picked him up in Sierra Village, and drove him back to Yosemite, leaving him at Yosemite Lodge. The taxi fare was a hundred and twenty-five dollars.

A day or so later, Stayner continued, he began to fear that he left too much evidence. He went back into Room 509 with his passkey and changed the sheets on the bed. Then he drove the Scout out of El Portal, back to Highway 49, and all the way around to where he'd left the car near Long Barn. At that point, Stayner took a number of personal items from the car and tossed them around the car, including the film and cameras, and then set the car on fire.

Once the car was burning well, Stayner said, he got back into the Scout and drove down to Modesto, where he threw Carole's wallet out on the street in an effort to confuse the police.

Rowlands continued scribbling frantically as Stayner told this story. There wasn't much chance to ask any questions, because Stayner was talking so much.

There wasn't much time to get into Stayner's background, but Rowlands elicited the remark from Stayner that he'd been aware of his rage against women since the age of seven.

"He remembered sitting in the car while his family was inside the grocery store, shopping," Rowlands said later, "and he had the fantasy of going inside the store and killing all the women checkers."

In fact, Rowlands got the impression that Stayner expected sympathy or at least admiration from Rowlands for restraining his killing impulses for so long.

"I got the feeling," Rowlands said later, "that he was playing the role of a good soldier, someone who'd put up with these urges for thirty years, and had successfully resisted them for so long." It was as if Stayner saw himself as some sort of hero for his long resistance, Rowlands said.

And there was another unusual thing about Stayner, Rowlands noticed.

"He talked about Bigfoot. He was obsessed with Bigfoot. He said he had seen Bigfoot himself."

Bigfoot, in fact, turned out to be Stayner's conver-

sational ploy in getting close to Joie Armstrong, Rowlands said Stayner told him.

"He said he talked to her about Bigfoot," Rowlands
said.

Once Stayner realized that Armstrong was alone, the
rage to kill overcame him, Rowlands said Stayner told
him. But Armstrong fought back, and by the time he'd
driven her body to the creek, Stayner said, he realized
that he'd left an enormous amount of physical evidence
behind—blood, hair, his tire tracks, even his sunglasses. It would only be a matter of time before the
police caught up with him, Stayner realized.

It was, he continued, different than when he'd killed
Carole, Juli, and Silvina. After that happened, he lived
in fear for weeks that the police would soon catch onto
him; in fact, during his first interview with the FBI in
early March, he was sweating, and felt he was obviously nervous. He couldn't understand why the police
didn't arrest him on the spot.

"I was a nervous wreck," he told Rowlands.

Subsequently he lost his appetite nearly completely,
losing 15 pounds in a matter of weeks. But no one
seemed to suspect him, Stayner told Rowlands; he
couldn't believe it. And when all the speculation about
Larwick and Dykes began to appear in the paper, Stayner said, he realized that he'd gotten away with murder.
That was when he wrote the anonymous letter to the
FBI, telling them where to find Juli Sund's body, he
said.

TWENTY-EIGHT

ROWLANDS'S 6:00 P.M. REPORT dropped like the bombshell it was on the assembled media in Sacramento. While they all knew that the FBI believed it had evidence connecting Stayner to all four murders, and there were reports from "sources close to the investigation" that Stayner had confessed, here was an actual in-person confession to a reporter.

Rowlands soon found himself the center of attention of a number of national news shows, including *Good Morning America*, *Burden of Proof*, and others. In each, Rowlands explained how Cary Stayner had personally confessed to him.

This, of course, was a defense attorney's worst nightmare: not only had a prime suspect waived his rights to an attorney, he'd given a taped confession to the authorities, had re-enacted the crimes on videotape, and had even spilled his guts to a television reporter. Could the situation be any worse?

Nevertheless, a week later, at his arraignment in U.S.

District Court in Fresno, Stayner pleaded not guilty to the murder of Joie Armstrong; it was apparent that two different cases would have to be brought against Stayner, one in federal court for Joie's murder, and another in state court for the murders of Carole and Silvina, and the kidnapping-murder of Juli Sund. Because those crimes had either taken place or began in El Portal, that made Mariposa County the most likely venue for the Sund-Pelosso prosecution.

In the meantime, law enforcement officials were digging through their unsolved case files, looking for similar murders to those of Joie Armstrong and Juli Sund; the decapitation motif was striking to many experts. Some said it indicated a powerful desire on the part of the killer to utterly control the victim; by cutting off the head, the victim would never be able to harm the killer ever again.

A number of similar cases cropped up in police files, including one decapitation murder of a woman near Lake Don Pedro, and a second close to nearby New Melones Dam. A third decapitation case was noted in Santa Barbara; what all this meant was that investigators would have to go over Cary Stayner's life for the previous 20 years with an excruciating attention to his exact whereabouts on specific dates. Indeed, many experts doubted whether the Sund-Pelosso murders were Stayner's first, as he claimed to Rowlands. The reality of serial killers was that most started far earlier than their late thirties.

And there was yet another mystery to be linked to Cary Stayner. In December of 1990, Del's brother Jesse had been found shot to death in his house in Merced. Cary had been at work at the time, but some now wondered whether that killing, too, was the work of Cary Stayner.

Stayner's assertion to Rowlands that none of the Sund-Pelosso victims was sexually assaulted turned out to be a lie, as most experts who study such killings predicted it would.

In fact, as was soon reported by a variety of news outlets, the usual "sources close to the investigation" contended that Stayner admitted raping Silvina Pelosso before killing her, and that he forced Juli Sund to perform oral sex on him for hours prior to leaving Room 509 of the Cedar Lodge early in the morning of February 16. Doubtless, too, Stayner had been seeking to have sex with Joie Armstrong when he attempted to overpower her; her fighting back made it impossible to remove her from the scene, which in turn led to his eventual capture.

In many ways, much of Stayner's life—at least as it was uncovered by investigators and news media in the aftermath of his arrest—fit the model of a typical serial killer, at least as defined by the FBI's behavioral sciences unit: Stayner had few, if any intimate friends; he drove an older vehicle that wasn't that well maintained; he held (and probably preferred) menial jobs that placed little responsibility on him; he liked to expose himself to women; and most of all, he cultivated the mask of sanity so well that nearly everyone who thought they knew him believed he was a "normal guy."

Also typical of serial killers was the rage Stayner expressed toward women; and while many experts doubted strongly that the rage began at the age of seven—which was four years before Steven Stayner's kidnapping—it is possible that male rage toward women begins at an early age. Many studies of psychopathic personalities in prisons have indicated that the essential "bonding" that needs to take place between mother and child never occurred in the case of psychopathic personalities, for whatever reason. The small child is utterly dependent on the parent for food, care, and most of all love. Thus the "abandonment issues" referred to by some experts have in fact engendered rage by males toward females that dates back to the earliest years of consciousness.

And what of Dykes and Larwick, the central "rogues" who had occupied so much of the attention of the TOURNAP people from almost the outset of the case? Larwick, of course, had denied any involvement in the crimes from the beginning; as for Dykes, "sources close to the investigation" reported that Dykes now admitted that he'd been fooling the investigators all along, partly by using what the investigators had asked him, partly by guessing, partly by weaving real, if irrelevant, things into the mix, and partly by finding out from pals on the outside what the FBI was asking *them*.

TWENTY-NINE

As the Stayner case winds its way through the courts over the next year, doubtless a number of questions that remain will eventually be resolved.

Not least among these are the forensic issues raised by the discovery of fibers linking Larwick and Dykes to the body of Juli Sund; and what about the mysterious calls to Wells Fargo Bank, inquiring about Carole Sund's accounts in the days following her disappearance? What about the ring some believed belonged to Juli Sund?

The FBI still wasn't able to rule out the involvement of others in the crimes claimed by Stayner. In this regard, the gamut of possibilities runs from a full-scale accomplice who had helped capture the three women in the motel room and tie them up, to the possibility that Stayner had left certain articles stolen from the trio in various places, where people associated with the "rogues" fell into the trap of picking them up. And there are obviously possibilities between those two extremes; as Maddock put it, the investigation into just what did happen will have to continue for many months to come.

Francis Carrington, among others, did not believe that Stayner acted alone. It would be, he thought, simply too difficult for one person to control all three women in a motel room. How could he tie them up with duct tape while holding a gun on them? To Francis, it didn't make sense.

In the middle of September, Cary Stayner, still looking for his movie of the week, contacted producers for the *Leeza* television show broadcast on NBC, offering himself for an interview. This was after the show had sent him a letter "offering him an opportunity to comment in efforts to assist in the Carringtons' quest for answers."

Leeza Gibbons, the show's star and producer, felt distaste at the prospect of giving airtime to a man who had admitted to such horrible crimes, but because she had already decided to feature Carole Carrington to highlight the lives of the victims, she felt obligated to give Stayner a chance to tell his side of the story.

A producer asked questions and took notes as Stayner talked; clearly, it seemed, Cary was still looking for recognition equal to that once accorded to his brother.

During the show, Leeza Gibbons read Stayner's remarks and asked Carole for her reactions.

"I just want to offer my heartfelt apologies for what

happened," Stayner told the producer. "The pain they [the families] feel and the pain I and my family feel, what everyone has gone through for what I did. Because I can't control myself, and their loved ones were there when I was dangerous, and I feel horrible about it."

Carole pursed her lips at hearing this.

"It's a non-apology apology," she said. "It's like saying I'm sorry I spilled soda on your carpet."

The only thing the Carringtons wanted from Cary Stayner, Carole Carrington said, was for him to tell the truth about what happened—all of it—when it happened, where it happened, and most of all, whether anyone else was involved.

THIRTY

BUT THE QUEST FOR ANSWERS wasn't limited to the Carringtons; Special Agent in Charge James Maddock and the FBI received a great deal of pointed criticism from the media for missing Cary Stayner so completely for so long. The criticism went up the chain, all the way to Washington, and if the Bureau had changed a great deal since the days of J. Edgar Hoover, there was one thing that hadn't changed very much at all: being at the helm when criticism was leveled at the FBI was not a good career move.

Officially, top people at the Bureau backed Maddock up; and whatever the real feelings were back at the J. Edgar Hoover Building on Pennsylvania Avenue, there was no denying the fact that Maddock and his agents had come into a high-profile case with literally nothing to work with.

Rather than the usual method of investigating— when one starts at a crime scene and works toward the suspects, Maddock and his people didn't even have that to start with. All they had was the mysterious disappearance of three people, without a clue as to where they had gone or what had become of them. Under the circumstances, the FBI did the only thing it could do: get the public busy looking for the car, and start at the other end of the pipeline, not the what, but the who.

It may indeed turn out that one of more of the "rogues" had some involvement in the crimes, however witting or unwitting; but one thing was sure, the Great Parolee Roundup of 1999 did net a number of people who were up to bad behavior. Their arrests led to still other arrests, and anyway it was looked at, that wasn't a bad thing in and of itself.

And as for overlooking Cary Stayner: while Stayner claimed to have been "a nervous wreck" during his first interview with the FBI, there's reason to believe that was only Stayner's way of trying to make his life story compelling to Hollywood. The way Rowlands described Stayner's demeanor is probably much closer to the mark: calm, deliberate, cool, relaxed. That indeed is the face of the typical serial killer—just like, as Joe Klass might tell you, the guy next door.